The Truth About Trust

THE SECRET TO THRIVING IN ANY RELATIONSHIP

Joi M. Ross

TRILOGY CHRISTIAN PUBLISHERS

TUSTIN, CA

Trilogy Christian Publishers
A Wholly Owned Subsidary of Trinity Broadcasting Network
2442 Michelle Drive
Tustin, CA 92780

The Truth About Trust

Cover design by: Jeff Summers

For information about special discounts for bulk purchases, please contact Trilogy Christian Publishing.

Manufactured in the United States of America

10 9 8 7 6 5 4 3 2 1

Library of Congress Cataloging-in-Publication Data is available.

ISBN: 978-1-63769-134-2

E-ISBN: 978-1-63769-135-9

Contents

Disclaimer

The following body of work was written as non-fiction. At its core, this book deals with common questions and commonly held views about "trust" and the role it plays in human relationships, as well as the role of trust with respect to the views and expectations we tend to have about life in general. It examines and questions the root cause of heartbreak and disappointment that many—too many of us—have experienced in relationships with other people (whether romantic, business, family, or friendship relationships).

Although the author has a strong spiritual foundation rooted in Christianity and a personal relationship with Jesus based on God's love and grace for mankind, and regardless of whether you share her spiritual beliefs or don't consider yourself to be spiritual at all, the principles in this book can absolutely help anyone seeking to have better relationships and experience greater joy in life. The author simply asks that you read this book with an open mind and an open heart and be willing to follow the practical steps for yourself.

It is absolutely possible to be free from constant disappointment and heartbreak in relationships. But it's virtually impossible to avoid it until you awaken to the truth about trust. The power lies within you. Lasting change, true freedom from disappointment, heart fractures, and heartbreak, is a beautiful journey from the inside out.

Dedication

This book is dedicated to my loving parents, who devoted themselves to providing everything they could to create a home environment where I could grow, feel safe, learn, and feed my curiosity and hunger for knowledge. They taught me about creation, the importance of developing a personal relationship with God, and the importance of giving my time, talents, and finances to produce value for other people and society as a whole. Those principles were then, and remain today, foundational to my life and have kept me grounded in the toughest of times.

Acknowledgments

Being an author wasn't something that I ever set out to become as a goal or dream. It chose me. I simply heeded what I felt was a "call" to share my story with the goal of helping others who've struggled with similar things. I'm grateful for divine guidance and instruction on what to say, how to organize the chapters, and for the courage to be transparent and vulnerable. Everything good in my life, every achievement, every accomplishment, every ounce of positivity and joy, as well as any positive impact I've had on others are the sole result of God's presence in me. I would not have been able to write this book without spiritual downloads, insight, and revelation.

I'm grateful to Charity Warren, who was my midwife on this project. She helped me push the content out of my spirit, out of my mind, and onto the pages. Her encouragement and insights were invaluable, particularly during the many moments while writing that I struggled with self-doubt. I believe we were divinely connected, and words are inadequate to express my deep love and gratitude for her.

I'm also grateful to my husband and parents for understanding my need to be transparent with certain parts of my life that include them and expose information that they wouldn't necessarily have chosen to share. Yet, in support of my need to write this book, they encouraged me to be open and share whatever details I felt necessary. I realize that they were being generous, even though they may have felt a bit uncomfortable at first. I appreciate their support.

I'd be remiss to not acknowledge the many years of wisdom, spiritual guidance, and friendship of my pastors, Gregory and Grace Dickow. I've learned and grown so much as a result of being connected to them for nearly twenty years and serving in various capacities at Lifechangers International Church under their leadership. I love and appreciate them deeply.

Last but certainly not least, I'm eternally grateful for my executive coach, the lovely Lisa Nichols (and her executive assistant, Margaret, who embraced me from day one). Lisa came into my life at the perfect time, like a bright light, a ninja, a "Yoda," and a rush of much-needed air and energy during the final stages of writing this book. A best-selling author, acclaimed transformational coach, and speaker who's touched millions of lives, Lisa continues to amaze me with her wisdom, humility, kindness, drive, and generosity. She pushed me and helped me to see things from a different perspective. She saw in me things that I didn't even see in myself. Her advice and suggestions—not just on my writing and speaking, but business and life in general—have been precious, priceless jewels! I'm blessed beyond measure to have Lisa in my corner. Lisa and Margaret are precious gifts from God. I'm eternally grateful for their support and encouragement.

Foreword

Joi Ross exquisitely navigates you through a journey of love, loss, shock, reconciliation, determination, and perseverance, all leaning on God's Word. Reading The Truth About Trust reminded me of all the heartbreaks that I experienced that required me to lean on my unwavering faith—my trust in God. I'm brought back to my moments of disappointment both in myself and/or in someone else or the circumstances and how I navigated from what felt like despair to determination.

Joi does a phenomenal job of illustrating what disillusionment can do to us and how to get back from it. The concept of understanding "the currency" of trust is such a powerful tool that Joi masterfully allows us to take a peek in her window of life, navigating financial despair, health challenges, relationship disappointments, and finding her way back to trust expansion, love, and grace.

And in this time and this season, when our perseverance, our determination, our trust, and our patience all feel as if they're being tested, The Truth About Trust is a definite must-read, a how-to, and a great reminder of who we all have the opportunity to be and become.

—Lisa Nichols
NY Times Bestselling Author
Celebrated Personal Transformation Guru and Coach
Founder of *Motivating the Masses*

Where is Your Trust?

Trust in the Lord with all your heart; and lean not on your own understanding.

Proverbs 3:5

During much of my adult life, the topic of trust is one that I've spent much time thinking about, struggling with, and praying about. And I believe God has given me revelation on what trust is, how He designed it to be used, and why so many humans struggle with it. I've learned a lot about trust in the "school of hard knocks." If trust were an ocean, you could say that over the past fifteen years in particular I've launched out into the deepest part without a life vest and learned many lessons that left me emotionally wounded and led me deeper into a conversation with God. Those lessons often came through heartbreak, disappointments, fractured relationships, emotional pain, financial challenges, and health issues as catastrophic as cancer itself. The pain, however, turned out to be a critical component of my journey toward a deeper relationship with God, a greater sense of empathy and understanding of others, and clarity about my purpose.

Within a two-year period, I went from a lifestyle of running and working out five days a week, being a fanatic about eating organic, avoiding processed food, and basically checking all the boxes in terms of what the "experts" say we need to be doing to be in optimal health, to sitting in my doctor's office during a "routine" exam and being told, "you have cancer." Talk about a surreal experience!

During that same period, my business was on a huge upswing, on target to hit a seven-figure milestone. I had opened a new office in Chicago, and we were in a major growth spurt. It was the best of times and the worst of times all at once. I felt like I was in a movie watching this happen to someone else. But the onslaught of medical exams and reports that followed convinced me that no, this wasn't someone else's life—this awful diagnosis had been given to me, a lover of God, a believer in the Bible and the healing power of Jesus, and a devoted church-goer, tither, and giver. And if that wasn't bad enough, shortly after that, my business lost two major contracts, and my personal finances—which by society's standards were in the range where people labeled my financial status a "success"—came crashing down. To top things off, my marriage felt like it was on life support. Simply put, I felt distressed, disillusioned, and disappointed. I kept hoping someone would come along and make it all go away! But no one ever did.

Trust—my entire foundation and everything I thought I knew about the Word of God and my spirituality—was shaken to the core. How could this be happening to me? I felt like my body had betrayed me, and life's hard knocks were shaking my faith. Nothing made sense. After all, I was faithful with my church attendance, gave well beyond 10 percent of my money to charity, and gave my most valued resource—my time— to those in need. I had actively served in my church for many, many years. I prayed and sought the Lord regularly for guidance and tried to live Christianity in my day-to-day interactions and not just let it be some "religious practice" of simply going to church and checking a box. And there I stood with a shrinking bank statement in one hand and a bad report from the doctor that read "Thyroid Cancer" in the other! And I thought to myself, Where did I miss the mark? I was waiting on God to do something! And I would later learn that God was waiting on me.

I stood there, in that corridor, the invisible place where heaven meets earth with unbearable hardships. It was in that sacred place that I began to really seek the Scriptures, to gain clarity on what they said about healing and trusting God. A new foundation had to be laid, and it began with my tears and brokenness. I cried. I prayed. And I waited on God to meet me where I was—and boy did He! In the chapters of this book, you'll see the revelations that followed. My hope is that by sharing my story of how my life's journey led me to have a deep desire to explore the topic of trust, and by sharing the truths about trust that I believe God opened my eyes to, maybe this will help enlighten others and help them avoid the pitfalls which inevitably come when we misplace our trust. I mean, after all, what is trust really? And do we know how to use it? Why do we end up being disappointed and heartbroken in relationships with other people, even when we put forth our best effort to be real and honest? Have you ever asked yourself these questions? I certainly have! If I can help one person, then it's completely worth sharing my story in a completely transparent way.

I don't profess to be an expert on relationships by any means. I'm not a psychologist, human behavior scientist, licensed theologian, or scholar. What I am is someone who has had many struggles and received many "downloads and revelation from above" (as I refer to it) that have set me free in many areas and opened me up to live and love more fully. I've been a lifelong student and learner of human behavior, spirituality, the Word of God, and I've experienced the power of going inward (spiritually and mentally) and upward (to God) for solutions and help instead of going "outward" and expecting other people to meet my needs. As much as humans might love each other, the truth is that humans don't have the capacity to meet each others' needs fully. This is something that took me over twenty years to learn, and even now, I often have to remind myself. I'm simply here to share my story—my journey—because it's what I was called to do. I believe there are others struggling with some of the things I've struggled with, and it's my life's calling to help lead others to freedom! My prayer is that, as a result of reading this book, people will feel encouraged, enlightened, and empowered to face and go through their own valleys in life, and come out stronger, better, and with an enhanced sense of freedom due to a deeper understanding of what it truly means to know God, trust God, and know your God-given power and how to use it. This understanding brings with it the power to transform from the inside out. I know because it happened to me.

My ultimate aim is to spark curiosity and awaken readers to the truth about trust so they can hopefully experience less disappointment and heartbreak, and have healthier, more fruitful relationships in every area of life, entering into each relationship from a place of wholeness, generosity, and standing firm in a place of being "unbreakable."

CHAPTER 1

Hidden Agendas

I, the Lord, search the heart...
Jeremiah 17:10 (KJV)

When I look back into my early childhood, trust was always something that was important to me, even before I could even define or understand the word "trust." Growing up in a pastor's family, I recall many challenging moments. During grade school, high school, and even long after I moved out of my parent's house, it was tough to establish good relationships and solid friendships. Often, people would want to get to know me and be my friend. But I would find out later that they were less interested in me, and they really were just curious about me being a pastor's kid and what it was like to grow up in a pastor's house.

Some kids often wanted to come to my house or ask me questions about my father. Few of them were deeply interested in getting to know me or be my close friend. They mainly wanted to know what a pastor's family was like. What was he like during his day-to-day life? What was he like when he was not at church or in a pulpit? What was our home atmosphere like? Was it like theirs? And when I was out with friends during junior high and high school, it seemed there were always people who didn't know me well who would constantly watch my every move as if waiting for me to do or say something "wrong." Like many young kids growing up in a highly restrictive household with many rules, as a teenager, I rebelled and tried doing many things that we were "forbidden" to do (smoking cigarettes, drinking, smoking marijuana, going to parties when my parents thought I was somewhere else, etc.). I'm not proud nor glamorizing that behavior, I'm just being honest about my upbringing. And when my peers would see me doing these things for the first time, they would often laugh and say, "Ah-ha! I knew it! You're not perfect; you're just like the rest of us!" I constantly felt like I was being watched under a microscope and rarely felt like I could trust people enough to just "be myself." Also, it seemed that people held me to a higher standard, which was something I never understood, and it made me uncomfortable. This caused me a lot of confusion and pain growing up. All I wanted to do was have close relationships with people that I could trust, who wouldn't betray me, and who had no deceptive or ulterior motives. I never really dis-

cussed this with anyone. I just kept it in my heart between God and me.

> Have you sometimes felt any of the following
> as a result of relationships with others?
> ✓ Betrayed
> ✓ Hurt
> ✓ Deceived (or lied to)
> ✓ Heartbroken
> ✓ Disappointed
>
> If your answer is yes, begin reversing this
> trend today by taking the action steps at the
> end of this chapter.

I figured that one day I would encounter people who
didn't have ulterior motives or hidden agendas. I would
have the type of deep, trusting relationship with another person that I so desperately wanted. I searched
for it in all of my friendships and relationships with
boys (and later men). And time after time, I would feel
betrayed, deceived, lied to, disappointed, and hurt.
This continued throughout my adult life until the Lord
started opening my eyes and taking me deeper in my
relationship with Him. He showed me that there was
nothing wrong with "other people," it was me (gasp!).
I needed to adjust my glasses, so to speak. I needed to
change my perspective of human-to-human relation-

ships. This was mind-blowing! I felt like, "what? Do you mean I've had this wrong my whole life? The problem has been *me? Wow!*" Talk about a humbling experience. I'm so grateful God woke me up. And I'll never be the same.

I grew tired of having my heart broken and of being disappointed in my relationships, and it occurred to me after much deep reflection, prayer, searching the Scriptures, crying out to God, going to counseling, and finally reaching a point where I was willing to be totally honest with myself and transparent with God. It occurred to me, and I believe it was a revelation; I had this "Aha!" moment! I believe God spoke to me and revealed the main reason why I struggled over and over again in my relationships—with family, male-female/romantic relationships, friendships, and even business relationships. I had this "knowing" deep in my soul, my gut, that I never fully understood trust and how it worked. And that lack of understanding was a huge reason why I often felt hurt, betrayed, or disappointed in my past relationships.

The Trust Exchange

The revelation that I received was that this world has currency (dollars, coins, material things that can be sold or traded), and God has His "currency." This world's currency governs all human-to-human transactions for goods and services. You go to work. Then, an employer pays you money for your labor. You own a business and sell services or products, and customers pay you money. You sell your jewelry or clothing online or to a clothing resale shop, and in exchange, they give you money. You get the point. That's how this world's system works. You give something and then get something of equal value in exchange. And while humans try to use this same philosophy in their relationships—I do something for you, you do something for me in exchange; I give you my trust, and you give me your trust in exchange—it never works out that way, and we end up being hurt, disappointed, and, over time, hardening our hearts and guarding ourselves to the point of not being able to have open, healthy, honest relationships. We even convince ourselves that we're better off by ourselves, not really letting people in or getting involved in deep relationships.

The thing is, in human relationships, the currency of this world's system doesn't work. It never has, and it never will. Contrary to popular belief and mindsets held by many in the United States (and other countries) during slavery times, "buying" and "trading" are concepts that were never meant to apply to people and human relationships. Even today, people are often confused and think it's possible to "buy" someone's trust by being generous and nice. I love the movie *Pretty Woman*, but it's fantasy. The whole notion of a man being able to "buy" a woman in terms of developing a deep trust relationship with her in less than one month is simply false. It's the stuff of great movies, but it's not the stuff of real life. Perhaps that's part of the reason so many relationships and marriages fail over time—unrealistic images in our head of what things should look like, belief in fairy tales, and misplacing our trust in people. Don't get me wrong; I'm an optimist and a believer in relationships; I just think our human perspectives on what a relationship should be like are often distorted.

I believe the reason that "trust" doesn't work in human-to-human relationships is that God created people, and He designed a system for us to operate in with respect to how we interact with and treat each other. Putting trust in human relationships is not part of God's system. God has a currency, just like this world has a currency. His currency includes things like belief, faith, expectation, desire, and trust. The Scripture says, *"Take delight in the Lord, and he will give you the desires of your heart"* (Psalm 37:4). *"Trust in the Lord with all your heart and lean not on your understanding..."* (Proverbs 3:5). *"Let God be true, but every man a liar"* (Romans 3:4, KJV). God created us to give Him our desires and trust, and He promised to fulfill desires and be faithful and trustworthy. Nowhere in this equation are we designed to put expectations on other humans to fulfill our desires or be completely trustworthy and faithful. I know this goes against much of what society tells us. But the truth is, particularly when it comes to relationships, what "society" tells us is often distorted and leads down a path of unrealistic expectations. To put it more bluntly, the one who listens and lives his life by what "society" says will surely find himself running into a brick wall or over a cliff at some point. This is because society is simply a collection of individual people who simply don't know everything, no matter how smart or intelligent or educated they may be. And since every person is unique, nobody can really tell another person exactly how to navigate. All we can do is share what we think and what we've learned or experienced. Only God, Creator of the universe, has all the answers. That's one of the reasons why it's so important to have a deep, personal relationship with Him.

The things in God's currency, like trust, belief, and faith, are only intended for human-Divine exchange. Our exchange with God, the Creator, the Divine, the All-Powerful. And God's currency doesn't work in this fallen world's system when we try to apply it to humans. You see, according to the book of Genesis, when Adam and Eve doubted God and instead believed Satan's lie, it activated or opened a portal to many consequences, including broken relationships and misplaced trust. The "sin" wasn't the eating, it was their unbelief. When sin entered the world, a system designed by the devil was activated in the earth (that system includes deception, lies, broken promises, selfishness, and pride). Because of this, we live in a world that operates on a system that's contrary to God's system. This world's system—this world's currency—will never produce the desired results because it's based on deception and lies. The Bible says that Satan himself is the "father of lies," so, naturally, everything that comes from him is deceptive. And because of Adam's fall, all humans are tempted to lie and deceive, which is why most of us (if we're completely honest) would admit that we have lied and/or deceived another person at least once at some point or another, even if our intentions were not "evil" at the time. The devil wants us to believe that we should put our trust in other people, and he wants us to buy into a lie that says trusting people is a "good thing." But that's not quite right.

Only when two people are able to truly love, appreciate, and serve each other out of an overflow of their own love for God and self, and from a place of generosity without expecting anything in return, can they experience a healthy, whole, satisfying relationship with each other. This goes for any type of relationship: business partnership, family, marriage, friendship, dating, etc. This is a matter of love, appreciation, value, and respect, not of putting total trust in each other or holding each other to a standard that no human being can live up to. Putting our trust in people will always lead to pain and heartache, which God never intended. God sent Jesus to set us free from pain and heartache (according to Isaiah 61:1).

Think of it this way: if you are going to an ATM machine to get money out, you need to insert your debit card to complete the transaction. And your debit card is the "mechanism" required to make that transaction work. Let's say you go to an ATM machine and you have money in your bank account, so you're thinking everything should be fine. You have your checkbook (I know, checks are old school, but go with me here for purposes of illustration). You try to insert your checkbook into the ATM machine to get money out, but it doesn't work.

You scratch your head and go to another ATM machine. You try to insert your checkbook there, and it doesn't work. Several ATM machines later, after trying the same thing, you're highly frustrated at best. You're frustrated and wondering, What the heck is going on? There's money in your account, so why can't you get it out of the darned ATM machines? You keep trying the same thing and getting the same result: no money.

You are saying to yourself, "Hey, why aren't any of these stupid machines working?" Well, guess what? *None* of those ATM machines are ever going to work because you are trying to use the wrong "currency" or mechanism. Until you use your ATM/debit card, the machines won't work. You can try to put whatever you want into that little slot, but it will only respond and produce the desired result when you insert a debit card. That's how it was designed.

This World's Currency

You cannot use a checkbook in an ATM machine and get cash out. It won't work. The ATM is not the problem. The problem is with you. It's essentially a "user error." It's due to your lack of knowledge of how ATMs work. Your expectation of the input-output process is flawed. No matter how many times you try, when you're trying to insert anything other than a debit card, it won't work, and you'll end up frustrated and disappointed.

It's similar with trust and people. Often, we don't understand how trust works, and we lack the proper knowledge of its use. Consequently, we end up being frustrated, disappointed, or heartbroken in our human relationships. We have tears, heart wounds, and soul wounds in our relationships with people because we are putting trust in them. We often enter into relationship after relationship, hoping things will be different. We think the problem is with "that person," and if we just find another person, a better person, we can avoid disappointment, broken trust, and heartache. And inevitably, we find ourselves being hurt, disappointed, or even betrayed again. This is true in families, marriages, friendships—all relationships.

Have you ever felt like you kept ending up in the same place of heartbreak, heartache, or broken trust, going in and out of relationships facing the same thing but with different people?

We sometimes have a tendency to go from relationship to relationship expecting things to be different because we change partners, friends, clients, or spouses. If you can relate to that, you're not alone! Begin applying the action steps at the end of this chapter today to change things.

In the early stages of a new relationship, we often hope and want "this" person to be different from "the others." Our hope builds up, only to reach a point where something happens, they break a promise, they tell a lie, or they commit an act that leads us to feel betrayed or deceived. And then it happens again: disappointment, heartbreak, and feeling dismayed because this time we really thought things would be different. Sometimes this cycle leaves people feeling bitter or thinking that there's something wrong with them or perhaps they're just meant to be alone. And that's sad because each of us was created to have healthy relationships with people; no one was meant to be an island. We often don't realize that the problem is not with other people (just as the problem was not with the ATM machine itself). The problem is often our lack of knowledge about what trust is and how it's designed to be used. Our perspective of human-to-human relationships is often flawed.

We often enter into relationships hoping to have a "trust exchange" with people. That is, consciously or subconsciously, we often have an "I can trust you, and you can, in turn, trust me" expectation. And that is what we believe our interactions with people should look like, particularly in our close relationships. If I show myself to be trustworthy, the other person will do the same. That's a common perspective. It sounds logical and reasonable in our minds. But the truth is, God never intended for people to be the holders of our trust. People are not designed with the capacity to hold our trust. Nor are we designed to be the holder of anyone else's trust. Because, even on our best days, there are going to be some things about us that are not trustworthy. This may sound harsh, and there's a part of our brains that wants to say, "That's not true! I can be trusted." But if we're brutally honest and transparent, we have to admit that even on our best days, those of us with the best of intentions have at a minimum told some form of lie or failed to make good on a promise in a relationship with another person. Whether it was a "white lie" or we concealed the truth. Or, at the time that we made a promise, perhaps we really intended to keep it, only to later justify in our minds why we needed to break that same promise. Either way, regardless of how we justify it in our minds, a lie is a lie. (Romans 3:4 [KJV] says, *"Let God be true, but every man a liar."*) Humans break their promises. It's just what we do. God knew that when He created us. And that's why He instructs us not to put our trust in people, because He doesn't want us to be hurt.

Love people—yes. And believe the best and hope for the best. But don't put trust in people. That's a truth that can be hard to swallow at first; it definitely was for me! But it has the power to transform us and how we respond to people. The one who embraces this perspective positions himself to be rooted in emotional intelligence, self-awareness, and a high degree of unconditional love and empathy toward others. Lasting change and true transformation is a process that always involves spiritual, mental, and physical components. The simple explanation is that we are mind, body, and spirit, and all three are involved in determining how we show up in the world, interact with others, and process situations.

Complete, total honesty and the ability to "make good" on a promise are critical for being trustworthy. And *only* God can do that 100 percent of the time. He alone is completely faithful and incapable of lying.

None of us are capable of living up to a standard of being 100 percent trustworthy. This is not something that we should feel bad about. It doesn't mean we're all evil and doomed to hell (thank God for that!). It simply means that we're human, and all humans are flawed. It's okay. And actually, the moment that we accept this fact, it actually frees us from the bondage, negative entanglements, and heartbreak we often experience when we put our trust in other people or even ourselves. It also frees us from having any hidden agenda or secret expectation or desire that another human will "finally be the one" to live up to an unrealistic standard of total trust. If the Creator of mankind said, "Trust only me," it's worth at least considering that He said that for a reason. Right?

Practical Action Steps

Please allow me to share with you some simple steps that have proven effective in my life in terms of experiencing freedom from focusing on whether others are trustworthy or have hidden agendas, and, instead, learning how to truly trust God and love people without being deeply affected or "crushed" based on what they say or do (or fail to say or do). I believe these will help you as well. In fact, I know that if you open your heart to God, these steps will absolutely work for you because God is no respecter of persons. What He has done for me He will do for you. Every positive outcome I'm sharing in this book is a prophecy, a projection of what can happen for you!

Step 1: Ask for wisdom. Acknowledge you don't have all the answers. (It's okay! Humility goes a long way.) James 1:5 says, "If any of you lacks wisdom, you should ask God, who gives generously to all without finding fault, and it will be given to you."

Pray this out loud: "God, you promised to give me wisdom if I ask. I'm asking you, in the name of Jesus, please open my eyes and give me wisdom. Show me what trust really is and how I should use it. Reframe my expectations of people to align with your Word and your Way. Please give me a new perspective on trust. Help me to understand my role in human relationships. Please remove any obstacles that would prevent me from hearing your voice or seeing things as you see them. I submit to you. And I thank you for hearing and answering my prayer. I receive your wisdom." Pray this sincerely, and insights will begin to emerge. Your perspective will begin to change.

Step 2: Seek knowledge and understanding. Search the Scriptures. Seek, and you will find. Visualize yourself going on a road trip with God or on a scavenger hunt to find hidden things. You're going to have fun on this journey!

Read the Bible; that's where the truth will be revealed to you. If you don't know where to start, I suggest starting with a simple Google search. Search for "Bible verses on trust," "Bible verses about trusting God," "Bible verses on trusting others," and "Bible verses on trust in relationships." Make a list of those scriptures, and then commit yourself to go on a journey reading each one. When you look them up, I strongly suggest reading the entire chapter that the verse appears in, so you can understand the proper context (i.e., who was speaking, and under what circumstances were they speaking/writing). This is critical because anything taken out of context won't give you the proper understanding. While you search and read the Scriptures, your eyes will be opened. Listen for God's voice. He'll speak to you as you read His Word. In fact, before you start reading, say a simple prayer, *"Lord, as I read, please reveal the proper meaning to me. Help me to understand what I'm reading. Help me to get out of this what you want me to receive."*

I'm excited for you! If you do this, you're going to have so many "Ah-ha!" moments.

Step 3: Forgive yourself and receive God's forgiveness for lies you may have told, actions you may have taken that harmed others, things you may have done (intentionally or without knowing) that left others feeling betrayed or hurt. God loves you tremendously. If you've accepted His gift of salvation through the blood of Jesus, your sins are completely forgiven. When God looks at you, all He sees is perfection. He sees you the same way He sees Jesus (He has given you the gift of making you "righteous," meaning that He's put you in right standing with Him, just as if you'd never sinned). He's not condemning you, so don't condemn yourself. Forgive yourself. Forgive others, everyone who has betrayed you, lied to you, broken a promise, "flaked out" on you, or caused you any type of pain or heartbreak.

Pray out loud, "Father, I thank you that you have forgiven my sins. I believe Jesus died for all my sins and shortcomings (past, present, and future), and He nailed them to the cross, never to be remembered again. I receive your forgiveness, and I forgive myself. Help me to see myself the way that you see me. I pray now for every person who has hurt or betrayed me in any way. I forgive them, and I release them from any bondage or obligation to me. I release them into your care and ask you to bless them. In Jesus' name. Thank you for hearing and answering my prayer."

Follow these steps as an ongoing practice until it becomes part of your nature. That is, until these steps become a part of how you automatically operate day-to-day, at the cellular level; until it's no longer something you view as "steps," but simply something you do as an ongoing way of acknowledging your human limitations and God's limitless love, wisdom, and power that's freely given to you for the asking. Don't worry if you don't feel any different right away. Keep doing it. As you follow these steps, you'll begin to think differently, and, eventually, you'll start to see a shift in your relationships with others—not necessarily because *they're* different, but because *you* will be different. I *highly* recommend that you incorporate this into a "daily practice;" take fifteen minutes each morning, or thirty minutes, or whatever you can devote. It will change you.

There are many good sources of inspiration and information. And I'm a firm believer in learning as much as you can from a variety of sources. But when it comes to total transformation and change that sustains over time, I've tried many things and can only offer you what has proven to work over and over in my life, in scientific studies, and in the lives of so many others I've observed through years of informal and formal research and counseling. And that is, hands down, spiritual transformation rooted in a personal relationship with God as Father, Creator, and lover of our soul. Nobody knows us better than He who created us.

CHAPTER 2

Square Pegs and Round Holes

The Lord is my Strength and my shield; my heart
trusts in him and he helps me. My heart leaps for
joy, and with my song I praise him.

Psalm 28:7

The good news is, while none of us humans are capable of holding another person's trust because we will inevitably fail, there *is*, however, one who is capable of holding our trust. One we can tell our deepest secrets to, and He'll never tell another living soul. One we can reveal our deep, authentic selves to without fear of judgment or condemnation and who will love us unconditionally no matter what. Someone who alone is able to not only be there whenever and wherever we need, but who will never, ever, ever hold our past against us. And who will never, ever, ever fail us or forsake us. One who *always* has our best interest in mind. That someone is Jesus. He knows us better than we know ourselves.

He loved us so much that He literally gave His very life for us. The Bible says a beautiful exchange happened on the cross that changed things forever! Jesus became what we were (separated from God because of sin) so we could become what He is (righteous, free from sin, one with God and perfect in His eyes). I don't know about you, but I'd have a really hard time agreeing to die for a close friend or even a family member (*sorry, friends and family! Just being honest here.*)

I sat alone in my room for months, trying to figure out my life after many years of heartbreak and disappointments due to "relationship issues." I was talking to my husband one day during that time, and he shared with me a revelation he believed he received from God. I stood there in the kitchen listening, my feet feeling heavy like blocks of concrete preventing me from moving, trying not to cry or reveal that I was feeling desperate at that moment for *any* sort of divine insight because I was about ready to throw in the towel on my marriage and every other relationship. I was wondering if he could see that I had been crying all night. Or if he knew the depth to which I was struggling and the deep questions in my soul. At that time, our relationship wasn't in the best place, and I hadn't been sharing with him my deep personal struggles and challenges. I hadn't told him I was in the middle of a major crisis and was questioning everything I had based my life on up to that point.

That's perhaps a story for another book, but that's where I was. It felt like a rock bottom place emotionally. With keen interest, I listened as he shared the conversation he had with the Lord about his struggles in various business and personal relationships. He explained that God spoke to him and said, "The problem is that you don't understand my currency." I remember standing there frozen, eyes wide open, being fascinated at the word "currency." *How odd*, I thought, *that God would use that word within the context of trust.* And then a feeling of warmth came over me like a cozy blanket as I thought about how awesome God is. He meets us where we are and talks to us in the language we can understand. My husband is what I would call a "techie," he's very skilled at math, engineering, technology, and the mechanics of how things work. He can take anything that's manmade apart and put it back together again, and explain how it all works. He's a numbers guy. So, of course, God would speak to him in words that convey numbers, mechanics, and logic. "Currency." It was perfect!

God told him, "You don't understand my currency."

So he asked God, "What do you mean?"

And God said, "Trust belongs to me. It's my currency. I never meant for it to be part of the world's system."

I was totally confused, and my head was full of questions, but because I was in such a fragile emotional state and didn't want my husband to know what I was dealing with, I just listened and said something lame like, "I'm not sure I understand." Under the surface, I was dying to know what he meant! And more importantly, I was hanging on every word, hoping that he would say something that would help me make sense of what I was convinced at that point was a "matrix" I was living in. He told me how God spoke to him and explained that trust is something God created for Himself, for people to give to Him and Him alone. And when we misplace trust by putting it in people, it's an inevitable setup for failure because we're expecting or asking people to do something that they're simply incapable of doing— holding our trust. People simply weren't created for that purpose. And when we put our trust in people, we're basically asking people to be God (which, of course, is impossible). I stood there, silent, listening to him and feeling like I was living in an alternate universe. It was like the movie The Matrix, with Keanu Reeves, where nothing in the visible world was what it seemed, and everything in the unseen world was what was *really* real.

During that season of my life, the spoiled little girl in me was feeling like I was living in a screwed-up world with screwed-up people, a bunch of liars and deceivers with cold hearts who couldn't be trusted; and somehow,

I was living in the midst of them, like some sort of a cruel joke. Okay, yes, I'm a bit dramatic. Perhaps I've seen too many movies, but you get the point. Ha-ha!

I was having a hard time with the whole concept of trust, even standing there in my kitchen that day, but the more I let it sink in the more it made sense. Putting total trust in humans is like asking a dog to sit and listen to our deepest problems and help us come up with solutions. As much as a dog may be referred to as "man's best friend" and as much as we may love our dogs and they love us in their own way, a dog is simply incapable of having an empathetic two-way conversation. It doesn't mean he doesn't love you; it simply means he's a dog, not a human. And he can bark, but he can't use human words to talk like we do. Only humans are capable of talking with words. And, in fact, it's unfair to ask a dog to be to us what only another human can be. You get the point, right? Humans simply are incapable of being to us what only God Himself is capable of being.

And only God Himself is capable of entering into a trust exchange with us. We put our trust in Him, He proves Himself capable (time and time again without fail) of being entrusted with whatever we give Him. He holds whatever secrets, desires, hopes, expectations we put on Him. And He gives back to us spiritual (unseen) and natural (tangible) responses—peace, joy, freedom from fear, solutions to problems, creative ideas, concepts, divine connections, financial increase, health and healing, wisdom. No human being can do that. No human being can touch the deep places in our hearts, souls, spirits, and minds that God can.

So there I was standing in the kitchen after crying alone in a room all night. Frustrated with my husband, a part of me thought, *You have no clue who I am or what I'm going through! Ugh! Why am I listening to you?* Still, I couldn't walk away. It's like the Lord was holding me there, putting His hand over my mouth and making me listen. You see, the Lord had been dealing with me on this same topic of trust. When my husband explained his revelation to me, a light bulb went off! So, I listened until he was finished, and then I walked away quietly, amazed. And I held what he said in my heart and began searching the Scriptures and asking God to give me wisdom and open my eyes to see what I had been missing when it comes to "trust" and my relationships with people. I wanted my own personal revelation from God. And God began to speak to my heart. He wanted me to understand that I am to put my trust in Him and Him alone. I had read this in the Bible before, but I realized I never fully understood what it meant—not in a real, living it out, sort of way. Until now.

Love people. Believe the best about them. Pray for people. But don't look to people from a trust perspective. This means, don't be disappointed or frustrated or angry if/when you tell someone a secret and trust them not to divulge, only to find out that they've told someone else. Or, when you open yourself up to a romantic relationship and the other person somehow betrays your trust, don't be surprised. Or, if a family member fails to be there for you in a way that you've grown up to believe family members should stand by each other, don't be angry with them, and don't feel like your world is crumbling if they seem to abandon you in your time of need. Humans will be humans. (And usually, the other person isn't intentionally trying to hurt you. Most likely, he or she isn't really thinking much about you at all. Ouch! There's a central character in the movie of their life, and sorry to break the news, but it's probably not you—it's them. Of course, there are exceptions, but generally, when people do hurtful things in relationships their behavior is rooted in some form of selfishness, being self-centered or self-absorbed. But that's a topic for another day.) Oh, and be *honest* with *yourself* about yourself. In any of these relationships, given the right set of circumstances, *you too* will let someone else down or betray their trust. Don't fool yourself or be so caught up in pride that you can't face that truth because when we get to a point where we're deceiving our own selves and pride sets in, we're truly going into a downward spiral, headed for an ultimate crash-and-burn situation. When we're at that point, we're in danger of making it really hard for even

God to bail us out. *"God resists the proud, but gives grace to the humble"* (1 Peter 5:5 and James 4:6, NKJV). Pride, like unbelief, is one of those things that acts as a repellant to God. It's as if we're telling Him, "Stay away! Don't help me! Don't come near me!"

In my 20s, I often wondered why in the Bible Paul said, "It's better not to marry." I now believe I understand a little better. I thought I trusted God, but after much introspection and many challenging years of relationships and marriage, I realized that I had coasted into a comfort zone, feeling like everything was fine because I was married, my husband made what society would consider "good money," and we didn't have any serious financial problems. We were living the life that society (and most of our family and friends) would describe as a "good life." But sometimes, when you're going through the motions and checking all the boxes (get an education, get married, get a good-paying job, get a house in the suburbs, etc.), it creates a false sense of security, and we can be sort of lulled into sleep. Like the *Walking Dead* (*yes, another TV/movie reference*), we can be living our lives every day, maybe even going to church and tithing on a regular basis, but not really, truly "living" or experiencing a deep, intimate relationship with God. And living this sort of life, checking off all the boxes that society (and even well-meaning family members) says will lead to happiness and fulfillment, is a trap. The trap is that we begin (consciously or, like it was for me, subconsciously) to put our trust in things and people instead of God.

After all, when things are comfortable, and you're not really pressed or challenged or facing any sort of difficulty, how do you *really* know whether you're trusting God? If you're able to do all the things you want to do, pay your bills, are in great health, and even help others in need because you've got a good income, how do you *really* know what it means to trust God wholly and completely to meet your financial needs? After all, living that type of life can deceive you into thinking that your husband, your job, your lifestyle, and your health are good because you made all the right decisions. *You* are good at what you do, so that's why you have a good income. *You* are good at making wise decisions, and that's why you haven't had any financial crises like others seem to. *You* eat healthily and exercise and avoid harmful food, that's why your health is good. After all, that's what society leads us to believe, right? It sounds so right, but it's oh, so *wrong!*

I didn't think that I was being self-reliant, but when things came crashing down around me and started getting "real" really fast, I was forced to take a deep look inside. And as painful as it was, I had to admit to myself and God that I hadn't been trusting Him with "my whole heart" at all. Not really. That was a day that everything shifted in my relationship with Him. My whole perspective on life shifted. And it's one of the best things that ever happened to me.

You see, trusting God with "all of your heart" doesn't mean trusting Him sometimes, and if you happen to fall in love, or meet some guy, then you can start looking to that guy to give you what you want and meet your needs. I know, all the fairy tales and movies we watch growing up tell us this—grow up, meet some rich, handsome prince (or even an average-looking prince with financial means), be swept off your feet, and live happily ever after. Or if you're a guy, meet some beautiful woman who's smart, sexy, knows how to cook, supports you emotionally and is capable financially, manages to have kids and keep her perfect figure, and makes wings and orders pizza when your friends come over to watch football. All of this while looking awesome, always being 'perky' and always being down for sex whenever and however you want it. If you find that in a woman, she'll make you happy and will never break your heart. No! That's not how it works. Not if you want to live your best, truly abundant life and experience all that God intended when He created you.

If we want true joy and fulfillment, we cannot split and divide our trust. We cannot give some guy (or woman) our trust, then leave another piece of our trust for God. That is not what He said, and that's not how

He designed things when He created the universe. The more that I began searching and reading the Scriptures and keenly observing the source of pain, anger, and heartbreak of many who have confided in me (either in a counseling or coaching capacity or simply as a friend), the more I began to see how a misunderstanding of trust (or rather, misplacing our trust) is central to most of the heartache that we experience—without even knowing it! In fact, I would say that *all* heartache and disappointment in human relationships is deeply rooted in "trust issues" if you pull back all the layers and examine the situation closely. In short, trust issues are rooted in trying to put trust where it doesn't belong and was never intended to go. Like trying to fit a square peg in a round hole, it simply will never work. And being awakened to this truth sets you free! For me, it was like a weight lifted off my shoulders that I never even knew was there. It was a sense of freedom that I desperately needed but didn't even know until I experienced it!

Practical Action Steps

If you want to be free from being brokenhearted, and if you want to be free from the pain and disappointment that's all too common in relationships with people, you can be! Follow these simple steps:

Step 1: Embrace humility and ask God to help you. In your own words, call out to Him. Be completely honest and transparent (He knows it all anyway, so there's nothing you can say that will shock Him). Acknowledge that you've been hurt, your heart has been broken, your relationships have been fractured, and perhaps you've tried to ignore it and "move on," but you've never really dealt with the pain. Let Him know you want to be free. Tell Him you believe what the Bible says, that Jesus came to heal the broken-hearted. I realize people reading this book are at different places spiritually, perhaps with different beliefs or no spiritual belief at all. If that's you, I urge you to open your heart and mind to discover who Jesus is. Embark on a journey to learn about Him. Read the Bible for yourself, starting with the book of John. And then open your heart, follow these steps, and see for yourself how it works. It's a personal journey of discovery that you really have to experience for yourself. Don't just take my word for it or anyone else's. Each human being has to take this journey for himself. It's a choice we're all given the privilege to make. All I can say is if the Creator of the universe offered you the option of knowing more about Him and experiencing His power in your day-to-day life, why would you not want to at least choose to find out who He is and what He has to offer?

Step 2: Receive. Accept God's help. You don't have to "earn" it; simply ask, believe, and receive. Open yourself up to His healing power to work in your life. Be willing to abandon and let go of any grudges or ill feelings toward others because of what they may have done to you or what they failed to do. And be willing to let go of any preconceived ideas and images in your head of what relationships with people "should" be like. To see any lasting change on the outside (including in your relationships), you must be willing to change and grow internally, expand your perspective of the relationships you're currently in, and shift your expectations of people. Expect healing deep within your heart and soul. Expect your perspective to change and be expanded, and allow it to happen; embrace it. It's not easy at first, but it gets easier over time and eventually becomes an automatic part of how you're wired internally. It's a process that requires you to continually be tuned in to your emotions and thoughts and "check yourself" and re-align when your emotions want to be in the driver's seat of your decisions.

Step 3: Commit to taking action. The Bible says, "Faith without works is dead," and "Blessed are those who hear the Word and also act on it." Be willing to move forward, starting today, by applying the Word of God and treating people according to what the Bible says, no matter what you've told yourself and no matter what you've been told by "society" (or even by the people closest to you) up to this point. Decide, it's going to be "His way" or nothing moving forward, and really mean it in your heart. You may feel like you're walking down a path into the unknown, but be willing to see where it leads you. Change isn't easy, but it's necessary for growth and for becoming the best version of yourself. Be willing to let go of old mindsets that contradict the best version of you.

Step 4: Search the Scriptures. "Seek, and ye shall find." Start reading the Bible, look in the New Testament, and see how Jesus treated people and what He had to say about how we should view and treat people. I suggest reading out loud. This will build your faith ("faith comes from hearing"), and the more faith you have, the easier it will become to put your trust in God. Keep an open mind as you read. Avoid looking for scriptures to "confirm" your preconceived ideas. Instead, be willing to let go of old ways of thinking and embrace the perspective and truths that the Holy Spirit reveals to you as you read. Even if you've read the Bible from beginning to end before, see this time as a new beginning. This is especially important if you've grown up in church or if you've attended church for a long time. That is because sometimes we end up adopting mindsets based on what we hear other Christians saying (and sometimes people mean well, but they don't necessarily have a true understanding of the nature and character of God but instead they have "religious" views and opinions that have been passed down from generation to generation). This is about really seeking for yourself, to get your own "download" directly from God and seeing it as mission-critical as if your life depends on it (because actually, it does).

Step 5: Take it day by day, one step at a time. Don't be hard on yourself. Simply wake up every morning, realizing that with each new day, we get a clean slate. Yesterday is gone, and tomorrow isn't promised. Each day, make it a goal to be kind to yourself and other people, be forgiving of your own and others' shortcomings and trust God to meet your needs and fill those spaces internally that no human will be able to fill.

Step 6: Document your journey and cultivate a lifestyle of gratitude. Get a notebook or journal. Write down the date and time that you decided to go on this journey of learning more about trust and God's currency. Write down the revelation and answers you receive from Him as you pray, listen for His voice, and read the Scriptures. Writing them down will help to "cement" the process (scientifically, it's proven that our brain chemistry is affected as we write things down, pen on paper). This will also help you on those days when things are challenging. You'll be able to go back through your notebook, remind yourself of what God has said and revealed, what you've learned, and what you're grateful for. And you can begin to thank Him for what He's done and for bringing you from "there" to "here." Gratitude for your progress will help lift your spirits and shift your thoughts toward positivity. Gratitude is also a pathway to experiencing more joy and freedom. Not only does the Bible support that statement, but having a grateful and thankful mindset has been scientifically proven to produce a host of benefits: more joy, happiness, fulfillment, and overall life success.

It's a process. Some days will be easier than others. You'll be tried and tempted to go back to your old way of viewing things and people, but stick with it. Make this a daily practice. Commit with all your heart. And I promise (no—even better—God Himself promises!) things will get better. You'll get stronger. Your heart will heal. You will show up differently in your relationships. And your relationships will be noticeably better than before!

CHAPTER 3

Ending the Cycle of Pain, Heartbreak, and Relationship Fractures

It is better to trust and take refuge in the Lord than to put confidence in man.

Psalm 118:8 (KJV)

I have a way of always tying things back to relationships. I have always been fascinated with male-female, parent-child, sibling, and friendship relationships. The thing is, there are certain laws or principles that operate in the universe (like sowing and reaping, giving and receiving), and God put these universal laws in place from the beginning of time. The universal laws of "trust" apply to *any* relationship! Universal laws are in full operation, whether we're aware of them or not, whether we believe them or not; and, we are subject to the effects of them, for better or worse. Like gravity. Whether you believe or understand it or not, if you jump off a building, you will fall to the ground. Splat! Similarly, there are universal, spiritual laws about thoughts and mindsets. Whether you're aware or believe it or not, what you think will surely influence what you experience in life. If you think you can't, you won't. If you believe you're a victim, you will often find yourself in situations where you feel powerless and helpless without a way out. If you believe, you can change outcomes. And, so it is with trust. Whether we believe the laws governing trust or understand them or not, they are operational. If we put trust in ourselves or other people, we will inevitably be disappointed and let down at some point. Whether we like it or not, that's a fact. It's a universal law of nature. To further illustrate how this works, allow me to share more of my personal experience.

Pain and Perspective

According to psychological research, most people at some point in their adult lives face difficulties or challenges emotionally (and in their relationships) due to things that can be traced back to childhood. That's probably because we have all experienced some form of dysfunction in our upbringing, even if we had "great" parents and lived in the best neighborhoods. People aren't perfect, and even the most well-intentioned parents and teachers will have some flaws that result in kids not getting 100 percent of what they need. I've heard spiritual leaders and teachers say that's how God divinely designed it. We weren't designed to get 100 percent of our needs met by people; rather, He designed us with needs that could only be filled by Him because He wants us to experience the sheer bliss and pleasure that only comes from a deep spiritual, loving connection that transcends the human experience. We are spiritual beings having a physical experience on earth, and until we connect with the Spirit (His Spirit), we can never truly be happy or fulfilled.

My upbringing was no different. I love my parents, and they were fully devoted to giving me and my siblings the best possible environment. That said, looking back to my childhood, there were many moments where I had deep hurts that I'm sure affected my overall perspective on trust in my adult relationships.

My dad was a pastor. He had a congregation of about 500 people or so when I was in grade school, but not a large staff. My mom was an elementary school teacher. She also worked tirelessly for the church (these days, she'd probably be considered "co-pastor," but back then, pastors' wives didn't really have titles other than "wife of the pastor." Hilarious.) So, when there were deaths in a family, or when people got sick or went to the hospital or were facing any type of situation where they needed counsel or help, they would call my parents. There was a designated phone line that rang to our house. Our phone would ring daily, sometimes constantly. And my parents would deal with whatever the issue was. They were very accessible to the church members. I understood that they were doing important work that God called them to do. But, at the same time, the demands of the church often resulted in them not really being there for me in the way that I felt I wanted them to be.

There were constant interruptions. Many canceled plans. Delayed vacations. Missed birthdays. Quality time was often cut short. One of my favorite things as a young child was to lie on my mother's lap while she rubbed my back. She gave the best back rubs! But inevitably, the phone would ring, and then I'd have to share her with whoever was on the phone. My mom was great, she'd usually keep rubbing my back while talking, but I was a jealous daughter and the youngest of four, so I was a bit spoiled and didn't want to share her with the world, and I'd always feel a little irritated that she couldn't just let the phone ring and give me "my" time. This wasn't a huge deal, but it sticks in my memory to this day as an example of how I rarely had "alone" time with my parents without their attention being split. And although I was often disappointed or frustrated, I didn't say much because I understood even as a child that they were helping other people who needed it. Although I was admittedly a spoiled child, I realized they were my parents and would always be there for me, even if it wasn't in the way that I felt I needed it all the time. So, I tried not to complain. I knew they loved me. And ultimately, I convinced myself that was all that mattered.

By the way, did I say my parents were great parents? They really were. I realize that these childhood memories, though, had an effect on my subconscious thinking about people and relationships in general. I questioned how people could be so demanding of people like my parents and expect so much with what appeared to be little regard for the amount of others' sacrifice. Were all people basically selfish, seeking to get more than they give, and prone to getting upset when others don't respond how they want? Did the fact that I often felt frustrated when my parents were called away to care for someone whose family member had passed away mean that I was selfish or insensitive to other people's needs? I didn't have answers, just questions. These were deep thoughts for a child. But I shook off the questions, went back to playing with my toys, and figured it would all make sense one day.

These experiences left me feeling skeptical in the back of my mind about whether I could trust anybody to be there for me the way that I felt I wanted or needed. I realize now that my skepticism had less to do with my childhood and more to do with the fact that I did not have a proper perspective back then of human-to-human relationships, and a five-year-old perspective placed things in my subconscious that affected my way of thinking even through adulthood. My expectations were a bit out of whack, and no person could ever have been able to live up to them.

The truth is, I was looking for my parents to fulfill a need inside of me that was impossible for them—or any other human being—to meet. Had they been with me 24/7, that deep, inner need would still have not been met 100 percent. And, in my adult relationships, people were never able to meet that need either because the need I had was rooted somewhere deep in my soul and could only be filled by God. The Scriptures say, *"He has made everything beautiful in its time. He has also set eternity in the human heart; yet no one can fathom what God has done from beginning to end"* (Ecclesiastes 3:11). There's a place, a "hole," or a "space," if you will, inside of each person's heart/soul that God put there for Himself. Only He can fill that space. It's beautiful when you think about it; He created a place in us where He could live because He loves us so much and wants to be inside of us, part of who we are, an integral part of our being; not just "out there" or "up there" in the external universe somewhere. A relationship doesn't get more intimate than that: to actually be a living, breathing part of another being!

Have you ever felt like there was a deep longing inside of you that no human being was able to fill? Or, have you ever felt that no matter how "full" your life was with human relationships or how happy you were in the moment, eventually, you'd have this longing inside that you couldn't seem to shake?

If you answered yes to either question, welcome to being human! If you want to resolve those feelings long-term, follow the action steps at the end of this chapter.

Human beings were never created to fill that space inside of us that God created for Himself. Nor were people created to "hold" trust. That's why we're not to "give" trust to people. It's unfair to them. And it's a setup for failure. We don't have the capacity. Imagine a small coffee cup and a gallon of milk sitting next to each other on the counter. You decide to pick up the gallon of milk and pour the whole thing into the coffee cup. You start pouring, the cup starts to fill up, then you keep pouring, and the cup overflows, and the creamy white milk starts running all over the counter and down to your dark hardwood floor until you've made a complete mess. You're probably thinking, *Okay, but why would I ever do that?* Exactly! Who would ever knowingly do that?

You would never try to pour a whole gallon of milk into a small coffee cup because you know it's not going to fit. A small cup can't hold a whole gallon of milk. Well, that's sort of how it is with humans and trust. Humans are like the coffee cup, and trust is like the gallon of milk. Try as many times as you like; whenever you're pouring your trust into another human and expecting him/her to faithfully "hold" (or uphold) your trust, you will end up with a mess on your hands eventually. But there are many other great things that a coffee cup can hold. It just can't hold a gallon of milk. And if we added a magical "bottomless container" to this picture that could hold whatever you pour in it, always with room to spare, God would be like that bottomless container. You could pour a gallon of liquid in that bottomless container, and not only would it hold the liquid, but there's also always going to be more than enough room to hold it. And you could add an unlimited amount of ingredients to the bottomless container, not just liquid, and everything would just blend in and eventually turn into something that smells and tastes really good! (*Can't you almost see it? Like a huge pot in the hands of a great chef! He keeps throwing in a bunch of ingredients, and when you're watching, it can seem like it makes no sense, but when He's done with it, it smells and tastes awesome! God takes everything we give him, all the good, all the ugly, and everything in between. And He creates something beautiful with it.*) The point here is that when it comes to people, it's important to understand their capacity and proceed accordingly for the best results. When we put on people what they're not capable of handling, the results won't be good.

I realize now that if I had really understood the depth of this trust thing early in life, it would have saved me much heartache. But that's like wishing you could go back to your five-year-old self and re-live your childhood with your adult perspective. It makes for a good movie plot, but it's obviously not possible. And what fun would life be if there weren't challenges and mysteries to navigate and life lessons to learn? The revelation I have gotten is that life is all about *perspective*. It's all about seeing clearly and trying to view things from a bigger, spiritual perspective, and, ultimately, God's perspective. Of course, we're not God, so how do we see from His perspective? We simply need to ask Him to open our eyes to see clearly and ask Him to give us wisdom. *"If any of you is lacking wisdom, let him ask of the giving God who gives to everyone liberally and freely, without finding fault, and it will be given"* (James 1:5).

Once we have the proper perspective of how we are supposed to use and give trust, and we realize it was not meant for humans, but for our relationship with our Father in heaven, then, and only then, can we begin to view our relationships with people differently and in a healthier fashion, and the wounds in our hearts can begin to heal. As I began searching the Scriptures and asking God to help me understand how to properly view my relationships with people, an image popped into my head. I saw myself as a water pitcher, and God pours into me whatever I need: revelation, wisdom, under-standing, knowledge, finances, peace, joy, etc. I look up to Him to fill me from that opening at the top of the pitcher, and He pours in and fills all the spaces within me. Nobody else can do it!

Then, and only then, am I able to pour out to the people I have relationships with. I believe this is the an-swer for all of us. So, whether it's a marriage, friend-ship, family, business, or any other type of relationship, the question to ask ourselves is *not* "what can this other person give me?" and it is *not* "can I trust him/her?" The question to ask ourselves is, "What do I have that I can pour out to this person or to this situation?" "What do I have to give?" If we feel we're running on empty and have nothing to give, that's a signal for us to look up to God and ask Him to fill us up.

When we approach relationships from this perspec-tive, we set in motion a spiritual law of nature. Whether we operate in it consciously or not, there is a law that as we give (or pour out), it comes back to us, not necessar-ily from that same person (in fact, it's rarely from the same person), but God sees to it that we get a return that's usually above and beyond what we gave. He gives back to us. Good things start moving around in the universe to come our way. We become magnets for good things. When we see ourselves this way, it impacts how we interact with people. When we look up to God to fill us up and then turn around and look out to the people around us from a giving perspective (rather than looking or expecting to receive anything from others), that changes everything! The Bible says that when we give, it is given back to us *"good measure, pressed down, shaken together, and running over"* (Luke 6:38, NKJV).

I realize this either sounds crazy or overly simple, depending on your mindset and whether you have a personal relationship with the Lord. And people who regularly attend church have probably heard Luke 6:38 countless times. But how often do we pause to think about what that scripture really means, especially with respect to our daily, human-to-human interactions? Just that little shift in thinking can open our eyes to view relationships differently and avoid being hurt or disappointed by people. Often, we get hurt because we have unrealistic expectations about what other people can do for us. We expect them to do things that they simply were not designed to be able to do! The resulting pain, disappointment, and heartache are something many of us have experienced over and over. One simple thing—asking God to open your eyes and change your perspective—can change this forever! Other people may not change, and you can't control that, but you will be different, and that will change everything for you.

The Laws of Capacity and Generosity

Back to the analogy of viewing yourself as a pitcher with an opening at the top (where you look up to God for all of your needs) and an opening at the side (where you pour out to others). You could say, then, that we live vertically (us and God) and horizontally (us and other humans). If we were pitchers, not only would water be poured in at the top, but water would evaporate up out of that spout. When we pray, that's essentially like our "water" evaporating up to God. He wants us to "evaporate" or send up to Him our desires, the deep matters of our hearts, our emotions, our pain, our struggles, our praise, our thanksgiving. As we do this, it makes room within for us to receive more from Him. From a trust perspective, we also look up (or out of our spouts on top) to Him and put our trust solely in Him. Once He fills us, water pours (or overflows) out of us to the people we interact with. And we always have something to give, which means we're always blessed! It's more blessed to give than receive. And God blesses us to be a blessing to others.

When you're always giving, you always have room to receive more of God's blessing, and you will always have good things coming into your life. If we're not filled, we have nothing to give; therefore, it makes it nearly impossible for us to play a proper role in our interactions with other people. Too often, we look horizontally (to people) for things that can only be provided vertically (from our relationship with the Creator of the Universe). And it produces disappointment, heartache, heartbreak, and relationship fractures. We might try to fix things by removing one person from our life and attaching ourselves to another, but without changing how we view the dynamic of human-to-human and human-to-God interaction, we're bound to repeat this cycle over and over.

I believe this is partly what Jesus meant when He referred to Himself as "living water." When we're in a close relationship with Him, He fills us to the point of overflowing. It's a continuous, never-ending flow of "living water." This means we always have something within ourselves to pour out. We're never lacking, never empty. Pause and think about that for a minute.

The first reported miracle Jesus performed was at a wedding feast when they had run out of wine. And He told them to get some empty water pots and fill them to the rim with water. They had to trust Him and just do what He said (even though it probably didn't make sense logically—how can filling pots up with water solve the problem of no wine?). But as they poured the water into the pots and filled them up to the brim, He then told them to pour it out. (Using my imagination here, when He gave these instructions, it must have required a certain amount of trust on their part because, logically, if you need wine and someone is telling you to pour water into a pot and then take that pot of water and pour it out to the wedding guests, it doesn't make sense!) But at that moment, when they acted on what He said and poured the water out, it turned into wine! And not only that, this wine was far better than what the guests had been served before. And I believe that's how He does with us. When we fill up with God and His Word, He works miracles and gives us "wine" to pour out. Sometimes it's us being a blessing to others; sometimes it's us having the solution we need in a work or business situation; sometimes we're in conversation with someone struggling, and we have a word of encouragement that penetrates their soul and lifts their spirits. Whatever the situation, we find that we have just the right "wine" for the occasion. How awesome is that?

We sometimes go through life without seeing the results we want, going through cycles of disappointment. And we may find ourselves asking, *Why am I not receiving the things I am praying for?* I believe deep, deep within me, that there is a law in the universe, whether we understand it fully or not, that is in effect. It is the law of capacity. In order to receive, we must first have capacity (remember the coffee cup/gallon of milk example?).

And in order to have capacity, there needs to be a constant flow going out of us, so we always have room to receive the new things. In order to receive, we must give! This makes no logical sense, and it certainly isn't what the world or society tells us. But it's true! And it works!

There have been times when I have felt stuck. I would pray and do everything I knew to do. In those times, I'd think I was trusting Him, according to my understanding at the time of what it means to "trust God." And I'd believe I was putting my faith in Him. Yet, there would be areas of my life where I was not receiving answers or getting results. When I look back over my life, *every* time I made a conscious effort to look deep within and consider "what do I have to give?" and then started giving (whether time, my talents, knowledge, money, or even tangible things in my house), God always would bless me in ways that I hadn't even been looking for. And I believe He has revealed to me this law of capacity—that is, He is always wanting to give things to us. *Always.* In fact, He's lined things up in the universe, and they are hovering over us, just waiting to come to us. But sometimes the timing is delayed because we don't have room to receive them because we're so filled up with other things. (Internally, we can be filled up with negative feelings, emotions, thoughts, unforgiveness, or opinions of ourselves or others that don't line up with the Word of God. Or sometimes, we're filled to the brim with the wrong relationships and associations.) And these "things" can block us from having any room to receive the things God wants to give us (or the people He wants to bring into our lives). Being intentional about pouring out and sharing the good we have with others, and looking up, going vertical, to receive more from God, produces many benefits, including expanded wisdom and capacity. And the wiser, the more full of love and grace, the more forgiving, the more peace and fulfillment we have on the inside, the less likely we are to find ourselves trapped in cycles of hurt, pain, and brokenness.

Practical Action Steps

Step 1: Be willing to expand your perspective. Acknowledge that whatever your view of yourself, others, and the world is right now, it's limited. Ask God to expand your ability to see beyond your current perspective. Believe that He heard and answered you. And start intentionally viewing things from multiple perspectives, not just your own limited point of view. This will have many benefits, with a primary one being that you'll likely become more empathetic and understanding of other people, and, in turn, you'll be more compassionate. Compassion was a primary aspect of Jesus' character and is often what moved Him. Compassion will move you as well, out of your comfort zone and toward discovering more about who you really are, what you possess that the world needs, and how you can make a shift toward tapping into what God has put inside of you and pouring it out to others. This takes your focus off of other people's actions and places it on your own growth and development.

Step 2: Embrace continual learning and growth as a lifestyle. As your perspective expands, develop a habit of putting your new and expanded way of viewing things into practice daily. One way to do this is when you encounter a situation with someone else that triggers a negative emotion or thought rooted in anger, frustration, irritation, disappointment, or fear, pause before you react. And actively try to view the situation from another perspective. Ask yourself some questions: What may have occurred to cause that person to say or do what they did? Could it be that they didn't have the capacity to be, say, or do what you expected of them at that moment? Remember, hurt people hurt others. Usually, when we're triggered by someone, they're dealing with emotions they haven't learned how to process. And that situation is actually revealing to us that there's something within us that we probably need to address that has nothing to do with them. Have compassion, pray for that person, and move on. The more you do this, over time, the stronger you'll become, the more control you'll have over your emotions and thoughts, and the less you'll be affected by other people.

Step 3: Enlarge your influence and impact. Pray like Jabez did in 1 Chronicles 4:9-10. Ask, "Lord, please bless me indeed, and enlarge my borders [my sphere of influence], be with me and keep me from evil, help me to not cause pain to others but to be a blessing to them." As you pray this and develop a deep desire for greater influence and impact, your whole world will begin to expand to allow you to do just that. Your desires will change, and you'll begin to have bigger dreams and visions. You'll begin to see yourself as a giver of what others need, as a solution carrier, a problem solver. The truth is, you are, right now, all of those things. You just may not know it yet. But as you focus on asking God to expand and enlarge your influence, you'll begin to see it. And once you see it, you can achieve it, and you'll be able to move through life more fluidly instead of getting stuck in destructive, hurtful cycles. At its core, this step is about looking for ways to give and pour out to others. It's about developing a "generosity mindset" and expanding your capacity to receive more of the good things God wants to give you. The more filled you are with things from Him, the more you'll begin to trust and look to Him, and the less you'll expect from people. Your life will become about what you can give out of your overflow, and you'll be having such a good time being generous you won't have much time to focus on what other people do or don't do.

CHAPTER 4

Looking Through Smudged Glasses

Your word is a lamp to my feet and a light to my path.
Psalm 119:105 (ESV)

Here is what I know for certain about God: He wants to give us the very best. He delights in giving it to us because He's a giver. That's His nature. It pleases Him, delights Him, makes Him happy to answer our prayers. If we abide in Him (put our trust in Him, live in Him, look to Him), and His Word abides (lives) in us, we can ask anything, and He will give it (see John 15:7). He wants to give us the best things because He loves us. He *is* good, and He *does* good! It is never the case that God is listening but simply refusing to answer our prayers (unless we're asking something that would cause Him to go against His Word. The one thing it's impossible for God to do is to lie or go against His Word). He is not sitting and saying, "No, I am not going to give you that!" That is never the case. But oftentimes, we are filled up with gunk! On the inside, we are like a car that desperately needs an oil change. Then, when the mechanic goes to change the oil, there is so much gunk that the oil has to be flushed out completely before he can pour the new oil in. Sometimes, the gunk inside of us needs to be flushed out before we can have room to receive all the good things God wants to bless us with. And the gunk is mainly our mindsets—our old ways of thinking need to be replaced with God's way of thinking. If we look to Scripture, it says that you can't pour new wine into old wineskins. If you do, the wineskins will burst, the wine will run out, and the wineskins will be ruined. No, you pour new wine into new wineskins, and both the wineskin and the wine are preserved (Matthew 9:17). We can't expect God to operate on our terms, according to our limited perspective, our limited ways of thinking. Thriving in life and relationships requires that we be willing to expand our view and drop old mindsets.

Realistic Expectations

It is important to see ourselves and others from the proper perspective. We put our trust in God, and He adds to us all the things we need (Matthew 6:33). People are not capable of doing that. We are to see people in terms of what we can give them, how we can help them, how we can make their lives better, and how we can add value. When we live from this perspective, we put ourselves in a position to receive a constant "inflow" from

God as we "pour out" what He gives us. We become a vessel. And when it flows this way, we don't get gunked up. There is always room to receive more. I've learned that having the proper perspective of trust is everything in relationships! It impacts our ability to receive from God and see His power show up in our lives. I have heard many ministers say, "God will give it *to* you if He can pour it *through* you." It's so true!

Assess The Accuracy of Your Spiritual Eyesight

When you have unmet needs, have you looked to friends, family, lovers, or others to help meet those needs?

Have you ever felt like you couldn't help others because you felt you didn't have enough for yourself and them?

Have you ever thought you had "faith in God" but found yourself questioning whether God cared or would come through for you when you were facing a challenge or crisis?

If you're like me and many others, you answered yes to at least one of these questions. Follow the steps at the end of this chapter to get a crystal clear vision that will forever change how you view yourself, others, and situations.

Each of us must decide what will rule our thought life. If we want to minimize the pain from heartbreak due to relationship fractures and failures, if we want to be able to continually receive what we need (and more), we must make a choice. We must decide that Scripture will trump our thoughts or any other "human" thoughts. If we want to see God's power in a mighty way in every area of our lives, we must choose to surrender to Him and eliminate any thoughts of our own that are contrary to His thoughts. He is going around seeking those whose hearts are fully His, fully devoted, fully turned toward Him, so that He can show up and manifest (display) His power in their lives.

This is *not* about going to church every Sunday as mere religious practice. This is about putting 100 percent of our faith and trust in God on a daily, minute-by-minute, hour-by-hour basis—expecting Him to fulfill His promises (to give us peace, provision, mercy, grace, solutions, clarity, and whatever else we need!). It is about getting to the point where you know everything good in your life has come from Him! Anything good, anything enhancing your life, has derived from Him. When you are there, in the most guttural part of yourself (in your core, in your gut), it produces a harvest in your life. You will automatically live a life of thankfulness and gratitude when you see how good He is. And it will change you forever. Because the more grateful you are, the more you'll attract good things and the more grateful you'll become. The old cycles of heartache and disappointment are replaced by an endless cycle of giving, receiving, being thankful, and receiving more. I don't know about you, but to me that sounds like an amazing deal! It's so awesome!

When I experienced God in this manner and developed this type of intimacy with Him, it literally began to transform me from the inside out. I was hooked and wanted more and more of Him. I stopped looking to people for help the way I used to, not because I had an attitude toward them, but because I only wanted to receive from the one true source of all things good. Nobody gives better gifts than Him!

When you sit with God and learn how much He loves you (everything He does comes from a place of deep love), it'll taste so good that you too will lose your appetite for anything humans may have been able to do for you in the past. This is what He wants. This is the type of deep relationship He wants with each of us. "*Oh, taste and see that the Lord is good; blessed is the one who takes refuge in him!*" (Psalm 34:8, NKJV). There is no room for fake trust once you've tasted this. If we're honest with ourselves, we can probably admit that even our best, closest friends have let us down and failed us at some point (and we've failed them). And we've probably let ourselves down at some point. All of those relationships pale in comparison to a deep, intimate, trust relationship with God.

Once we're living and swimming in the deep waters with God, experiencing His faithfulness and His goodness, we won't want to lean on our own human understanding as much. It's sort of a reflex or automatic reaction on our part—the more we experience His goodness, we'll want more of Him, and we'll begin to seek Him more in every area of life. Then He'll direct our paths, and He'll lead us into blessing after blessing. Just like in Scripture, when He led the children of Israel out of Egypt to the Red Sea and into the promised land. Or when He instructed Elijah to go down to the brook, and when he got there, the Lord had provision there, waiting for him! He will lead us the same way. And when we follow where He leads, the provision will just show up, and we'll see the manifestation of His power and blessing. That's when we know we've moved from "simple religion" and into a "deep relationship" with Jesus. There's so much love and freedom in that type of relationship with Him. And no heartache. God loves you and wants to bless you. He is looking for those who have pure hearts and those who trust Him with all of their heart.

Become a "Magnet" for God

Imagine God hovering over the earth or the atmosphere! Imagine Him literally going throughout the whole world, hovering. If you've ever been in an airplane, over a city when it's dark, you can see little, tiny lights shining through the darkness. And, although it's dark, the tiny lights shine bright enough to be seen from thousands of miles high. I believe this is how God sees us. When our hearts are His and our trust is in Him, fully and completely, there is a light that goes off—like a little magnet. And, God goes looking for that light.

"Aha!" He says to Himself. "This is a person that I can really show up for; a person I can reveal myself through; a person I can bless abundantly, beyond her wildest dreams!"

Please don't misunderstand. I'm not saying that He won't show up for other people. But you open yourself up to experience a much more glorious manifestation of His power when you give Him your whole heart and all of your trust. You will see His hand at work in your day-to-day experiences in a very practical way. You'll say, "Oh, wow! This had to be God!" You start to see the above and beyond, the miraculous show up in your day. That is one of the benefits of completely and totally surrendering our hearts to God.

We must have the right perspective on this whole trust thing in order to have healthy relationships. Know the importance of putting all our trust in God. And take trust out of the equation when dealing with people. Remove it all together from our interactions with people.

This is the only way to give God the "*all*" type of devotion and trust He deserves.

Practical Action Steps

Changing our perspective is sometimes easier said than done, mainly because our brains store memories and "code" things into our subconscious based on past experiences. The good news is, there's a vast body of research and evidence on the human brain that clearly shows that our brains can be reprogrammed. We can change our perspective. Know that you're not alone. You don't have to try to figure out how to change on your own. God is willing to help you. He wants to help you. He's just waiting for you to ask Him. He doesn't want to "force" Himself on you. If you want to shift your view of things to match His view, His way, and have all that He wants to give you, you're halfway there simply because you desire it! Here are some steps I took to jump-start the process.

Step 1: Ask for Help. You can pray this simple prayer right now, "God, I believe that your way is best for me. I believe you have plans for me that are good. I want to put 100 percent of my trust in you. I want my heart to be yours. I'm not sure I know how to do that. Please help me. Please guide me. Please speak to me and open my ears to hear your voice. Please teach me how to lean on you, how to trust you. And please teach me how to properly view people—the way that you view them. Open my eyes, my ears, and my heart to you. Help me to see and hear clearly. I believe that you're listening, and my prayers are reaching you because you're not seeing my flaws and shortcomings. You're seeing me through the blood of Jesus because I'm covered by His blood. I expect positive transformation and a new way of thinking, and I thank you for showing me the way." When you pray this, believe it with all your heart. *See* Him listening and answering. And trust that you have received what you asked in that moment, in the spiritual realm (and it's just a matter of time before it manifests in the physical realm).

Step 2: Don't Worry—Be At Peace. Once you pray this prayer, believing it with all of your heart, be at peace. Begin to follow these simple steps—start reading your Bible. Start attending a Bible-teaching church on a regular basis (either online or in-person), and keep your eyes and ears open. Expect to hear from God. And you'll start to hear His voice. And people who can help you will begin to cross your path (divine connections). Your eyes will start to open as you commit to these simple practices. Make a decision to make this a way of life, putting Him first. And once you begin to do this, you'll start seeing a change on the inside. Your thoughts will slowly begin to shift, and your perspective on things and relationships will start to shift. It's a process, but stick with it, and you'll be amazed at the results!

Step 3: *Choose* God's Way. If you don't belong to a church that's committed to teaching the Bible, may I suggest that you find one? Also, you will see great results by focusing on your thought life. One thing that has changed my life dramatically is my Pastor's *40-Day Fast From Wrong Thinking* book and Podcast series. You can sign up for free. It's convenient, only takes five minutes a day, and you'll look back and say, "this is one of the best things I've ever done!" I'm confident because that was my experience. When you sign up, you'll start to receive a daily email in your inbox with simple teachings on a common thought we all have had (for example, "I'm not good enough" or "Things will never change") and a few simple Bible truths to combat that thought. As a companion to the book, there's a corresponding audio/ Podcast link, so if you prefer to listen rather than read (for example, on your daily commute), you'll have that option. Each day for forty days, you'll receive an email with a thought and a Bible-based counter-thought. This will help you begin to clearly identify "trick" from "truth" in a practical way. At the end of the forty days, your outlook on things will have shifted, and you will be changed on the inside. And, as your thoughts go, so goes your life. To sign up, simply go to www.gregorydickow.com/fastfromwrongthinking or download the

Gregory Dickow Podcast. It's free! It doesn't cost you a thing and only takes 5-10 minutes daily. You'll be so glad you did this!

Changing your thoughts is huge because our mindsets dictate our outcomes. You can research it for yourself, it's both scientifically proven and explained in the Bible. To help you develop a growth mindset and experience lasting freedom and more joy in life, I've created a guide, *10 Growth Mindsets Essential for True Freedom*, as a companion to my book *Break the Cycle of Temptation, Addiction and Guilt: From the Inside-Out*. You can download it for free at https://freedomjoiross.com. It will help you begin to break free of mindsets that may be keeping you stuck in unhealthy relationships.

Step 4: Be accountable to someone. This is not a journey to walk alone. Find someone who's further along in this journey and who knows what you're going through. This is different from a best friend or family member you may feel you can talk openly with. You're looking for someone rooted in Scripture, someone whose life God has transformed, who has spiritual wisdom, coupled with experience, and can help you tap into your spiritual power. This could be a friend who's deeply rooted and grounded spiritually, a spiritual counselor through your church, or even a therapist or coach outside of church who is trained to help guide people through a transformative process (preferably someone who respects your faith). Talk to this person about your commitment, your struggles, and what you want for your future. Ask him/her to hold you accountable and help you. I'm a firm believer in the benefits of coaching, counseling, and therapy. These tools have helped me tremendously. You can google to find board-certified therapists and even Christian coaches or counselors in your area for either in-person or virtual appointments or simply use this link to type in your zip code and find someone near you: https://connect.aacc.net/?search_type=distance.

I have helped many people and would love to help you in your journey. I believe God delivers us out of things so we can then turn and help others who are struggling in those same areas. My past experiences, lessons, and pain can be used as a bridge for your progress. You can visit the products page of my website, https://joiross.com, for free resources or contact me directly. I also have a library of additional resources not posted on the website that I'd be happy to share with you. My motivation is simple. I believe I'm called to do what I'm doing and help as many people as I can by sharing what I've learned, what I've researched, and what has worked for me and others.

CHAPTER 5

Spiritual Currency: A Mindset Shift

He said to them, You are from below; I am from
above. You are of this world; I am not of this world.

John 8:23

The world operates on a mindset that says things like "tit for tat," "scratch my back and I'll scratch yours," or "treat people how they treat you." There's a currency system that works according to society's rules, and there's a valid place for that. But there's also a spiritual currency, a system designed by the Creator of the universe. God's system does not work the same way or according to the same rules of society. As humans living in this world, it is very easy to get tripped up in the world's way of seeing and doing things and in a monetary system of dollars. There are very few things in life that are free. Capitalistic society says: go to school; get as much education as you can; get a job; get a job making as much money as you can; buy a house; get a car; have kids; buy more stuff; rack up debt and worry later about how you'll pay it back.

When I was coming out of graduate school, the general mindset prevalent in society at that time was, if you could work your way into a corporate leadership or management role with a six-figure salary, you would know you've "made it!" But what I've discovered is: that whole mindset needs to be thrown out the window! It is flawed and, more importantly, detrimental to our ability to fulfill our true purpose on earth and see things from God's perspective. That mentality lulls people into a false sense of security. Also, that mindset is very limiting—after all, what does society's definition of a "good standard of living" really mean? Good according to whom? What does any of that mean when you think about a God who is infinite? A God who created the universe and everything in it? There are *no* limits in Him! And for those of us who believe in Him and put our trust in Him, we serve a God who is all-powerful. There is no greater power than His power. And when we accept His gift of salvation through Jesus' death and resurrection, He puts His Spirit in us. Think about that; we have His power inside of us! We have God-power, and He is all-powerful! If we have His power, that means we have the power to create and to bring into the physical world those things that exist in the spirit realm. The ceilings society says we should shoot for are false!

In God, in the spiritual realm, there simply are no ceilings! Work, get married, go to school, get a job—marry and have two incomes and feel good about your "success." *No!* That is this world's system. Get a house in the suburbs (or a gentrified city), get a dog, then pop out a couple of kids. Then what? Feel good that you "made it"? And wait 'til retirement when you can sit and do nothing, and then die? No, no, no! Don't get me wrong, I'm not saying there's anything wrong with going to school, getting a job, getting married, having kids, or any of those things. But God has so much more in store for us. He has such a greater purpose in mind for us. Getting married, having a "good-paying job," and acquiring material things alone is not the purpose for which we were created. In fact, that mindset can be a pathway to selfishness because it's primarily focused on "me"—my marriage, my family, my income, my social and financial status. What's missing in that equation are key questions that speak to higher ideals related to our being three-dimensional beings. What value can we produce for society? What is our assignment in terms of being part of the "whole" creation? Beyond working and earning money, what else are we to be focusing on? How can we contribute to solving societal problems? Before we were even born, God had already mapped out

His unique plan and destiny for each of us—one that goes far beyond material things (see Jeremiah 1:5 and Jeremiah 29:11).

The "Matrix"

Society's mindset and "rules" regarding how we should live life is largely a matrix, a false reality. And when we adopt the matrix mentality, we can't see what's real. The Bible says the things we can't see with our natural eyes are actually more real than the things we do see (2 Corinthians 4:18). In other words, the spiritual realm is more real than the natural realm. If you haven't seen the movie *The Matrix*, I highly recommend it. During the film, Morpheus (played by Lawrence Fishbourne) was the main person who had discovered there was a "real" world behind the fake one we live in day-to-day; and he was the leader of those who decided they no longer wanted to live in the fake world. The rulers of the matrix were on the constant hunt for Morpheus and all those who followed Morpheus because they wanted to keep people blinded from the truth, and Morpheus and his crew were on a mission to destroy the matrix. Morpheus was recruiting Neo (played by Keanu Reeves). Morpheus offered Neo a pill but told him, "If you take this pill, your eyes will be opened, and you'll never be able to go back." That's how it is with us and our relationship with God. We have the power of choice:

THE TRUTH ABOUT TRUST

we get to decide whether we want to live in the matrix and by the rules of society, or whether we want to see beyond the matrix and live a life beyond what we can imagine, tapping into our spiritual power. Once we take the "pill" of accepting Jesus as Lord and the Bible as the Word of God, our eyes are opened to a new world—true reality—and there's no going back. I decided I wanted all that God has for me, and I want a deep relationship with Him. I want my eyes to be open to see from His perspective, and I want to know the difference between what's real and what's fake. My eyes have been opened. Society's fake promises and fake definitions of success never lead where we are led to believe they will. It's an illusion, a trap that any one of us can fall into (and it's easy to get caught up in that trap).

It can happen to any of us, even "loyal" church attenders and those who read the Bible regularly. Even they can fall into the trap of saying and thinking to themselves, "I trust in God," while subconsciously trusting in the stuff they have, in a reality and mindset that society has fed them, in their spouses, or in their education or pedigree or the number of commas and zeros in their annual income. Often, it's not until we have some losses that we realize we haven't trusted in God the way that we thought we were. We were trusting in this world's system, trusting in the matrix.

Similarly, people who pride themselves on being knowledgeable and intellectual can fall prey to trusting in their mental capabilities. This plays out in ways like people having a false sense of superiority over others because of the books they've read, the classes they've taken, or the schools they've graduated from. Sometimes, this plays out among those who consider themselves to be "religious" or "theological scholars." You know, those who pride themselves in quoting Bible verses and giving super deep, religious responses to everything. I liken these people to the Pharisees who are described in the Bible as the people Jesus encountered who always were fixated on "right" and "wrong," and "dos" and "don'ts," and who felt morally superior to everyone else because they were well versed in the Scriptures. Ironically, those same people are the ones who Jesus described as hypocrites.

The point here is, what we *think* we know because of all the books we've read, or all the scriptures we've memorized, can create a false sense of security, and we can find ourselves trusting in our own knowledge or intellectualism instead of trusting in God. And just like all the other things (money, relationships, careers, physical possessions), no amount of intellectual knowledge can withstand the challenges of life. Inevitably, when we've trusted in our knowledge, we'll encounter something in life that we simply are unable to comprehend, something that leaves us baffled, something for which there is no logical explanation. Those times present an opportunity to look deeper into the possibility that just maybe we don't know as much as we think we do. Maybe there are truths that can only be revealed in the spiritual realm as we open ourselves up to God and look to Him to be the source of our wisdom. Don't get me wrong; I'm a huge fan of education, reading, learning, personal development, and growth. I'm not knocking any of that. I am, however, saying that nothing in this world (including books and other forms of acquiring knowledge) is worthy or capable of putting total trust in. Even the Bible itself requires our reliance on the Holy Spirit to reveal the true meaning. When read out of context or sheerly as an intellectual exercise, we will inevitably have an inaccurate perspective of what we've read (again, I refer to the Pharisees because that's exactly what their primary issue was, and why they never understood who Jesus was). We could say that the Pharisees were essentially caught in the "matrix" of their own false sense of intellectual and religious superiority.

The bottom line is that there are so many things vying for our attention and presenting themselves (falsely) as things we can rely on, things that we can build our life's foundation on, things that will weather any storm, whether it's money, relationships, tangible possessions, or even our education and intellectual knowledge. But putting our trust in any of those things will inevitably lead to disappointment and disillusionment because none of those things were designed to hold our trust. Have those things if you'd like, but don't trust in those things. Furthermore, removing any sort of expectation of others, with respect to giving you those things or celebrating or supporting you as you acquire "things" will definitely save you from unnecessary heartache and pain.

Practical Action Steps

The question is, how do we awaken to the things "outside of the matrix" and begin to see and more deeply experience the unseen, the intangible things, the things that are more real than the things we do see? How do we acquire that type of wisdom and spiritual sensitivity?

Step 1: Desire a spiritual rebirth. In John 3:3 (KJV), Jesus said, "Truly, truly I say unto thee, except a man be born again, he cannot see the kingdom of God." He also said, in verses 5-6, except we're born spiritually, we can't enter into (experience, or understand) the kingdom of God, and what is born of the flesh is flesh but what is born of the Spirit is spirit. The things of God cannot be seen or understood until we first come freely to Him and accept His love and gift of salvation through Jesus. Once reborn, we become "new creatures" (we're literally the same on the outside, but our spirits are reborn, and there's an internal awakening that allows us to see and understand the supernatural). Then, begin to walk in your new identity as a reborn daughter or son of God, and expect His power and Spirit in you to awaken and become a dominant force in guiding your decisions and transforming your perspective and mindset as you yield to Him. You'll begin to show up differently in your relationships with others. And when you're facing situations and challenges, before you automatically react, it will become easier and easier to pause first and ask yourself some questions like, what's really going on here? What am I not seeing? As you begin asking God to help you see situations (and people) from His perspective, He'll answer. Don't rely solely on your logic or intellect because your mind is only one aspect of your whole self. It can only provide partial information.

Step 2: Believe God. In Isaiah 35:4-5 and Isaiah 42:6-7, God promised to provide light and open the eyes of the blind, and lead us out of darkness so we can see clearly. In Christ, we have sight and no longer have to live in darkness. But we have to believe this. You can be given a gift, but if you never accept or acknowledge it, it just sits in a corner unused. Every day, confess and acknowledge, "Because I have the Spirit of God living inside of me, I have wisdom and insight, and I have the ability to see the unseen and discern the real from the fake, the truth from fiction, and I will not be deceived because I have light within me and where the light is, darkness can't exist. Thank you, God, for sight and light." This is a process. But the goal is to develop a habit of doing this daily and being constantly mindful that you do have this inner power. Over time, this will simply become a natural part of who you are and how you operate without any "effort."

Step 3: Tune in to the voice of God and your intuition. We all have a built-in mechanism to discern the truth, and that's our intuition. Our intuition is in touch and in sync with what's real, with the unseen and spirit realm. It's that "thing" that we sometimes refer to as a "gut feel" or a "voice within" that speaks to us and directs us to do this, or avoid that, or leave from this place, etc. Our intuition warns us of danger and also guides us toward the good things that the universe is trying to get to us. The more we pay attention and learn to quickly respond to that inner voice, the easier it becomes to discern what's good for us and what's not, and the easier it is to see through the matrix. Fill up on the Word of God, and then trust your gut!

CHAPTER 6

When "Loss" Becomes the Best Win Ever

All things work together for good to them who love
God, and to them who are called according to His
purpose.

Romans 8:28 (KJV)

Sometimes those situations where you feel your back is against the wall and everything you thought you believed in is being tested can turn out to be the best thing that ever happened in terms of your personal growth. A job loss. A health crisis where no amount of money in the bank can fix it. The end of a significant relationship. Death of a loved one. Of course, when you're in the middle of a situation like this, it's hard to see how it can possibly be turned around for good. But it can! In fact, God promises to take all things and turn them around for good to those who love Him and have been born again into His family by accepting Jesus as Savior and Lord (Romans 8:28). A common misconception is that God "causes" all things. That's not true. Things happen for a variety of reasons. But He will "turn" all things for our good, regardless of the cause.

Were it not for situations like this, for many of us, our eyes wouldn't be clearly opened to the matrix—the mindsets we've unconsciously adopted from society and the false senses of security we've unconsciously constructed in our lives. Things we've put our trust in (and even made them idols, false gods). That was me! I loved the Lord. I maximized my education. I went to Corporate America. I moved my way up in leadership, setting and reaching financial targets that society had taught me would result in a certain "successful" standard of living. I wanted that standard of living. I told myself, "I'm going to start my own business and be all that I can be!" And I did. And my business grew. I was financially rewarded. The more I made, the more I tithed and gave far beyond 10 percent of my income. I felt good that I was able to give and help others. Yet, I wasn't aware that my career and business "success" had created this sort of false security, a false safety net in my life. I really thought I was trusting God. After all, I had been in church literally all my life, and, except for a few wild and crazy years while in college, I had gone to church almost every Sunday all my life. (*My college experience is a whole topic for another book. God saved me from so much!*) I believed the Bible was the Word of God, and I considered myself a Christian. Life was good.

And then, there was a shift. Things started changing in the world, and it had a major impact financially for my clients. They started drastically cutting their budgets, which meant consulting firms like mine found themselves with drastic budget cuts. In some cases, programs were cut altogether, which meant the loss of contracts completely. I hit financial challenges that were so severe that they broke me—not just financially, but in my core! In my soul. I went from a place of not having to really think about whether I could afford to purchase something and being able to go wherever I wanted and do whatever I wanted (total financial freedom) to wondering how I was going to pay my bills. I felt like there had been an earthquake and the ground underneath me was shifting.

This shook me at the core and caused me to go into deep conversation with the Lord—and with myself! And my reaction to this personal crisis (confusion, sadness, frustration, self-doubt) made me wonder what I had really been putting my trust in. I went on a quest for wisdom and knowledge. I wanted to *really* know how this whole "trust thing" with God works. I wanted to know *His* system and *His* way of doing things. I had read and heard before that "He gives us power to get wealth" (see Deuteronomy 8:18). But I hadn't really thought deeply about it because I had wealth. Or so I thought.

When you are shaken to the core by a financial crisis (or any crisis), it will cause you to wonder. Especially after being a long-time tither, a giver, and faithful church attender (often twice a week!). When things shift from you being the person that people look to for financial help, to *you* being the person who's wondering, *How are my needs going to be met?* When you're looking at your bank account and the numbers aren't saying what you need them to say, when something like this happens, it can cause you to do some serious, deep soul searching. And deep Bible searching. And deep questioning.

Have you ever:
- ✓ Followed society's "checklist for success," only to find after you went through the steps that it didn't bring you the success or happiness you thought it would?
- ✓ Entered into a relationship or marriage thinking you'd be "happy ever after" or "financially secure ever after" only to be disappointed later?
- ✓ Had a loss of money, health, or people in your life that left you questioning your faith?

If you answered yes to any of these questions, you will benefit from taking the practical steps at the end of this chapter.

While I was in a dark financial valley, I started to remember all of the excellent teachings on finances I had been exposed to in my church. I was so grateful that God had planted me in a church where the pastor was fully committed to equipping people with deep knowledge about God's love, His giving character, and His way of doing things. No religious man-made rules and regulations, *strictly* Bible and how to walk this Christian life out, day by day, step by step. I began to pull out my notes from financial seminars, teachings on finances, and everything I could get my hands on pertaining to God's way of handling finances, receiving financial harvests, and God's financial system, His way of doing things. And I committed myself to eliminate any thoughts contrary to God's thoughts in the area of finances. Also, I began going deeper in the Scriptures to learn more about God's love. And as I began to really believe God's amazing love for me, on a very deep internal level, something amazing happened: He freed me from fear and anxiety! Perfect love really does cast out fear! Just like the Bible says in 1 John chapter 4. A calmness and peace began to come over me, and even though the circumstances in my life hadn't changed yet, things were different. I was different. I was no longer freaking out, but I had this "knowing" deep on the inside that everything was going to be okay, and not just okay, but things were going to be better! This was more than simply "positive thinking" or "hoping for the best." Something had shifted in my core. I had a deep peace, an inner knowing that great things were in store for me, even before anything began to change on the outside.

And I made a decision to stop all the "chatter" and questions in my head on how this financial tragedy could've happened to me (that's what it felt like, tragic; like I had gone from a fairy tale life into someone's nightmare). Instead, I just decided to believe God, no matter what the circumstances looked like. I wasn't going to put my trust in what I saw. And I really wanted to just trust God and not be afraid of how my needs would be met. Literally, as I saturated my thoughts with what the Scriptures say about God's love, I found that one day, I simply didn't have fear anymore! Miraculously, I didn't have to try to pray it away or chase it away. I had just stepped into this "no fear zone." I felt free! Little did I realize that step into the "no fear zone" would launch me where I needed to be in terms of a new perspective on finances. I started giving even more (even though it didn't make any logical sense). And eventually, my business started to turn around (with little direct marketing on my part, which I knew was a blessing from God). When I began to stop stressing and worrying and started giving more and more (of my time, talents, and money), my phone started ringing, and unexpected projects and contracts started coming my way with no effort on my part but to simply respond and say "Yes! My firm can do that!" And my bank accounts started to increase. I realize now that I had stepped into an unseen, supernatural river where the blessings of God keep pouring in as we constantly pour out (and I mean, pour out past the point of questioning; simply giving whatever the Holy Spirit says to give even if it doesn't seem "logical" or rational to the human brain).

During this point in my life, God would just speak to my heart and say "give 'x' amount to this person," or "give 'y' amount in the offering at church"—and it would always be an amount that seemed crazy to my human brain. But I'd trust Him and do it. Little did I realize, He was leading me down a path of planting seeds to reap the harvests He knew I needed. It's so counter-intuitive to give more when you're facing a situation where you desperately need something!

I had pushed past the tithe mentality and stepped into the "whatever you say, Lord; whatever I have you gave me, so as far as I'm concerned, it's all yours anyway" zone. Let me correct myself. I didn't do this. It was the *Lord's* doing: His work in me. All the water (the Word) that had been pouring into me for years was, all of a sudden, overflowing and turning to wine. I was forever changed. My eyes were opened to the reality of what God wanted to do through me: like projects and programs to advance His kingdom that He wanted me to fund; like lives that needed to be touched that would require finances, time, and talents that He wanted me to give; and like people who need to hear the gospel who would only hear if preachers are sent. And He wanted me to help send them.

And oh yeah, by the way, my needs would also get met in this process. This is a by-product of the financial flow He's designed: from Him to me and out to the world. This is a total paradigm shift, a mindset shift from the way I previously viewed finances and financial blessing. It's so not about me at all, and totally about His divine plan and purpose for mankind, and the role I am to play in it. *By the way, I don't believe this paradigm shift is just for me. I believe this is what He wants for all people. He wants each one of us to be awakened to His plan for finances. He wants us to be lifted out of the matrix.* If you're reading this, and right now your finances are upside down, and you have more bills than money to pay them, please *know this:* my testimony is a prophecy for you! God wants to use you to be a blessing to others. He just needs to know that if He gets it to you, you'll do with it what He wants done.

Throughout that process, I also had to be honest with myself and deal with my feelings and thoughts toward people. Instead of looking to my husband, parents, or anybody else in my life to provide what I felt I needed financially, I believe God was wanting me to shift my perspective and get rooted and grounded in His reality instead of society's reality. I learned through that period in my life that, regardless of whether you're married to someone who society deems "successful" or not, whenever you begin to look to that person to meet your financial needs, it will inevitably end in disappointment. God wants to be our source. We may be blessed to have a person in our lives who wants to do things for us financially, and that's great. Be grateful for that. But never forget that people are not your source. God is. This perspective shift has helped me to be extremely grateful for all the people in my life who choose to do things for me, but never to expect it or get mad when they don't because I'm not confused about the true source of provision and blessing. That freed me and healed me! What God has done for me, He will do for you! He doesn't play favorites. He loves us all the same. He's not a respecter of persons. He simply wants each of us to trust Him wholly and completely with everything we have. And when your heart is wholly His, with respect to your money, the universe will bring financial increase to you. With respect to your health, you'll have fewer health problems and will be strong and healthy, defying your chronological age. With respect to your relationships, you'll have more fulfilling relationships with less heartache. You will be like one of those little lights shining on earth, creating a magnetic force that attracts blessing and success. Get excited about it. Expect it. And brace yourself for the ride!

If, or I should say *when*, you find yourself in a situation, a "valley," where it looks dark, where it seems that you don't have nearly enough (time, money, strength, etc.) to meet your needs, and you feel that you're sinking without a life vest, what's *actually* happening is that the universe is presenting you an opportunity. It's a blessing in disguise. It's time to get excited and to begin expecting something awesome! It's in those times that you're forced to "hit pause" and critically think about your life, the direction you're going in, the things you believe in, the things you've been trusting in, and it's an opportunity to "course correct." Without an opportunity to course correct, we can continue blindly walking down paths that aren't going to lead toward fulfilling our purpose, experiencing joy, and experiencing abundance and freedom. And for many of us, for whatever reason, it's only in these rock-bottom places that we awaken to the still voice and the power within us that's been longing to bubble up, but which we've suppressed all of our lives (usually unknowingly). But when faced with a crisis, what's in us begins to rise up and scream, and if we listen and hearken to it, we'll open ourselves up to experience a life and a relationship with God that's more beautiful than what we previously imagined.

As I'm writing this book, the world is in the middle of a historic pandemic. And the pandemic has literally caused us to "shut down," be still, and hit "pause" on all of the activities that once filled our days. Almost everyone I've interacted with during this time has had this one thing in common: we freaked out and felt extreme discomfort during the first few months of the pandemic because there were so many unanswered questions and we felt as if life as we knew it had been flipped upside down and there was nothing we could do about it. It was a very challenging time, a time of questioning, a time of emotional and mental stress, a time of pain, and a time of anxiety and worry. But then, for those of us who submitted and realized that this was something we had no control over, a beautiful thing happened. People started turning to spirituality. To prayer. To meditation. Seeking God for wisdom and answers. Questioning why they were put on earth and whether they were living up to their calling and fulfilling their purpose. This questioning and seeking has led, for many, to a renewed sense of purpose. It has led to changed thinking. To new perspectives about life and how we spend our time. To a more minimalistic, spiritual way of viewing things instead of a consumption-materialistic-based mindset. To a mindset of giving and serving others instead of a self-centered perspective. People began rising up to help care for the elderly and the most vulnerable among us. Churches, who were forced to close their doors, began thinking about the true mission of the "church," to love and care for people and not just gather large crowds on Sundays to collect an offering.

We were all forced to look at some harsh truths about ourselves and the society we've been living in, with respect to racial and social injustice. And this is something that, were it not for the pandemic and most of us being in our homes watching the news, seeing the death of so many people of color, and the uprising of Black Lives Matter and other groups protesting against injustice, may never have happened. We may never have believed that racial and social justice were still unresolved issues had we not seen the horrific "real-time" unedited footage of brown people being killed and brutalized for things that non-minorities would be given a slap on the wrist for. Harsh truths. Painful truths. But out of all of this pain, something beautiful is happening. People are beginning to educate themselves and learn more about racial history. (That is, not the sanitized version of history we were taught in school, but real history and the hard-to-digest truths about intentional slaughter and mistreatment of certain races and classes of people by those who saw themselves as superior and who built their wealth literally on the backs of the people they were oppressing. When these people were later forced to change the laws, they looked at those same previously oppressed people as if something was wrong with them or as if they were lazy or somehow lesser because they couldn't seem to amass wealth despite the fact that literally the laws and societal systems had blocked them and their ancestors from fully participating in the economy for hundreds of years.) There is healing and forgiveness and change that's emerging as a result of these ugly truths coming to light on the global stage. We are, essentially, in a global situation of being given an opportunity to question what we believe in, what we put our trust in, and what mindsets we've historically held on to that we need to let go of. As I write, I'm hopeful that there will be a global spiritual awakening that results from all of this. That remains to be seen, and only time will tell.

If you're reading this book and feeling a bit unnerved or uncomfortable right now, consider it a good thing. It means that there's some part of you that recognizes there's something beyond your current perspective or way of living. Something better that awaits you on the other side. It's a necessary discomfort that's a prerequisite for growth.

Below are some steps you can take to turn things around in the face of any mountain, challenge, or situation that causes a sense of significant loss or pain. Whether the problem is financial, health, relational, emotional, or mental, these steps will help you climb over, around, or right through that situation into a place of greater wisdom, victory, strength, peace, and power.

Practical Action Steps

Step 1: Be still. When facing a major loss or disruption, your mind may start telling you, "Just do something, quick!" or "Don't think about it, find something to forget or numb the pain!" Those are normal reactions that are linked to our built-in "flight or fight" response mechanism. And it's linked to our natural tendency to want to take control, especially when it appears that things are out of our control. Although you may be tempted to start taking action right away, resist that urge. Force yourself to just pause and "be" for a while. You want to quiet yourself and all the chatter in your head so you can create an internal environment within yourself to align with your intuition and hear the voice of God. When facing extreme challenges, there's usually a lot of noise: opinions coming from other people, voices in our own heads, both conscious and subconscious, and it can be difficult to hear that still, small voice on the inside that's trying to guide us. Shut out all the other voices and listen for that small, still voice. It's connected to the supernatural realm and knows things that your conscious brain does not. So get somewhere quiet, away from everything and everyone, breathe deeply, and ask God, "What am I not seeing? What do I need to know? What do I need to learn? What's the first step that I should take right now?" He'll tell you. Whatever He says, act on it. Don't try to overthink it. It might be challenging or even feel weird at first. It's like a muscle that you develop. The more you do it, the easier it becomes, and eventually, it'll become something that's natural and easy.

Step 2: Go vertical—look up and look within. The wisdom you need during this time will come from above and from the Spirit of God within you. Avoid looking out, around you, and comparing your situation with other people's. God has a specific plan for you. Look up, expect wisdom, expect help, expect a solution, expect everything you need to get through this challenge to come from above. It may very well be that your solution includes other people or resources, but even then, it will require you to be focused above, on Jesus, and He will bring you in touch with the right people and keep you away from the wrong ones. What this looks like day-to-day is literally blocking some time (preferably first thing in the morning), to pray, read scriptures, and quietly listen for God's voice. You can know that it's His voice when what you hear is rooted in love. Because God is love, and everything He says and does is grounded in love and aligns with Scripture. God will never say something to you that condemns you or contradicts with Scripture. It's important to study and know what the

Scriptures say, so you'll have clarity. Clarity is essential for making wise decisions. When faced with a sense of deep loss, pain, or heartbreak, you definitely want to make wise choices as you move forward.

Step 3: Look for the good—for the opportunity. There will always be things that can go wrong. There will always be an option to focus on the negative. If you look for and expect the worst, that's usually what you'll see and receive. Opt out of negative thinking and negative expectations. Instead, choose to look for the good (even though you may be facing what seems like the worst situation you've ever encountered). This will help you identify all the things you have to be grateful for. And a heart and mindset of gratitude will expand your capacity to receive. It will activate your faith. And faith is what moves God and causes supernatural forces to work in your favor. Some refer to this as "the law of attraction."

Step 4: Be intentional about gratitude and giving. As you begin to focus on what you have to be grateful for and look for the good, your understanding of God's generosity will deepen, and you'll grow in your understanding of the truth of your own capacity for generosity. Remember, you have God's Spirit in you. So if He's generous (which He absolutely is), that means you are too. You might feel tempted to close yourself off from others or become selfish during times of crisis. That will not serve you. Pushing past that and intentionally focusing on others and how you can serve them will accelerate your path forward. It will set you on a course toward walking in the victory that God has destined for you. It's how His kingdom works. It's counter-intuitive to the "matrix," but we're not called to live in the matrix. You can literally give your way out of a financial crisis and have more wealth on the other side. I know. I've experienced it. And, it's a biblical principle. If it worked for me, it'll work for you. There's a spiritual law of "sowing and reaping" in Scripture. If you need money, sow it, and you will reap a financial harvest. If you need a friend, find someone who's lonely and sow friendship (be a friend to them), and you will gain friends. If you need joy, do something to brighten someone else's day, and you'll be happier. When the harvest comes, it usually won't come from the same source where you planted it, but keep your eyes open and be alert because it will come and usually from somewhere least expected.

Gratitude and giving are like muscles. We can develop these traits, and they become stronger and stronger the more we operate in them. If you start making it a habit to write down between one and three things each day that you're grateful for, it will have a huge impact. Doing this each day habitually has scientifically been proven to literally change your emotions and brain chemistry. You'll begin to feel more joy, look for more good, and eventually, you'll become more focused on looking for opportunities to give more because you'll want others to experience the joy of receiving and being grateful! It's an ongoing cycle that becomes part of your lifestyle. And you'll look back and discover that you're a more positive person than before, with more "bounce-back" ability. And it all starts with a few minutes of intentional gratitude and thankfulness each day.

CHAPTER 7

Villains and Superheroes

...whoever hears these sayings of Mine, and does them, is like a wise man who built his house on the rock [a solid foundation], and the rain descended, and floods came, and winds blew and beat on that house; and it did not fall, for it was founded on the rock.

Matthew 7:24-25 (NKJV)

Shortly after I thought I had gotten over the financial crisis, my business was booming and was on track to hit a record year. I had leased new office space and hired several new staff, and things were going great in that part of my life. I had some stress with the new office, new staff, and growing business, but that was to be expected. It was "good" stress—growing pains. I was feeling really good about being on the verge of reaching another major financial milestone in the business. I felt a sense of achievement. And, with my newfound perspective on finances, I was even more excited about all the different things I would be in a position to give money to. I could play a larger role in funding my church's outreach activities, give to different charities, help more family members, etc.

Then, like an icy snowball coming from nowhere and hitting me in the head, I was hit hard with a negative health report. I never had health problems before! I had done everything that "society" tells us. And I bought into the mindset that says, "If you do this or eat this, or avoid that, you can expect these great health outcomes." I worked out regularly (and with my improved financial condition, I had hired a personal trainer and was looking and feeling my best!); I shopped at Whole Foods and similar stores, read the labels on my food, ate mostly certified organic, avoided genetically modified and chemically enhanced foods with antibiotics, and so on. I was checking almost all the "boxes" in terms of what society says we should be doing to maintain good health.

But one day, after a routine office visit, I received a phone call that the doctor wanted me to come in to discuss the results of a test. I had just gotten off the treadmill and had gotten dressed and was getting ready for a meeting later that day, and I remember thinking, *Hmmm, that's odd. They've never wanted to discuss results in person before.* So I had a hunch it was something important, but I was not expecting what was to come. There

I sat in the doctor's office. My usual female doctor, who I really liked, was out, and another doctor was there. A man that seemed smart but wasn't what I would call a "warm" person. He seemed to lack the "people" skills to match his intellectual skills. I tried to strike up a friendly conversation when he walked in, just to loosen things up. But he was what I would call "stiff." I thought, *Hmmm, okay. He's gonna be a tough nut to crack.* Because I'm in the communication business, I try hard to connect with people and develop a good rapport. He didn't seem interested in that at all. I watched his lips move while he sat down, ignored my small talk and attempts to make a personal connection with him, and calmly said, "Your results are back; you have cancer." It was as if he had said, "Oh, I see you had chicken for dinner last night, that's good," or something equally as unimportant. I felt like I was outside of my body looking down on the whole thing like it wasn't really happening.

In fact, I laughed out loud and said, "I'm so sorry, please excuse me. It *sounded* like you said I have cancer."

And he looked at me almost without expression and said, "Yes, that's right. You have thyroid cancer."

He wasn't my normal doctor; she was out of the office. I wanted to scream and hit him with something! I was so taken aback by his seeming lack of concern. I was in shock. And all I knew to do was what I always do; I went on "auto-pilot" mode and asked a bunch of questions to get the "facts" and not let my emotions take over: "What does this mean? What are my treatment options? What's the worst-case scenario? What if I choose to do nothing at all? Are you sure about the results?" And then I calmly said, "Okay, thanks, I don't have time for this right now I have a meeting to go to." And I left.

Still feeling in shock while driving to my meeting, it started to hit me; and, I felt the tears well up in my eyes. But I told myself, *It'll be okay, I'll get through this, don't fall apart. Go get a second test and a second opinion, and pull yourself together and get through this meeting.* And that's what I did. I went to my meeting, calm and focused. I think I even secured a new project during that meeting. Then I went back to the parking lot, got in my car, said to myself out loud *"What the hell just happened? Whose life is this?"* And then, I cried all the way home. But when I got home, I had decided this was something I needed to deal with emotionally *before* talking to anyone about it. I told my husband but no one else. And I rehearsed to myself exactly how I would tell him beforehand. The last thing I wanted was for him to fall apart. I wanted to portray confidence. I got this. I'm not worried. This is just a blip on the screen of my life. No worries. (I thought, *If I kept telling myself that, everything would be okay.*) And that's exactly how I conveyed the message to my husband: very matter-of-factly. I said something like, "Hey, I received some weird news from the doctor today. I'm still processing it but wanted you to know he said I have thyroid cancer. But don't get freaked out. Just pray for me." And he did right there on the spot, and then I walked out of the room because I didn't want to give room for emotions to take over, and I certainly had no time to stand there and fall apart. I'm not prescribing this, I'm simply sharing where my thoughts were and how I reacted to give you a glimpse of what this whole experience was like. Honestly, looking back, I think I was probably still somewhat in shock when I told my husband and I just wanted to process everything on my own without any external opinions or influence.

My pastor had been teaching a series on "getting in the cocoon" (the "cocoon" being the place where caterpillars *must* go in order to reach their full destiny of butterfly status). In life, the "cocoon" is that secret, quiet place of getting alone with God and letting Him do His work in us. Although the "cocoon" can feel uncomfortable and even lonely, it's necessary in order for us to reach our full potential and fulfill our God-given destiny. So, I decided that was exactly what I was going to do. Shut out all external "noise" and go into a zone, into a cocoon, where it was just me and the Lord.

For weeks, I didn't really talk to anyone. I was in deep prayer and asked the Holy Spirit to lead me and tell me what steps to take. Following His lead, I researched everything I could get my hands on regarding the type of cancer I had been diagnosed with, including the top five places in the country that were considered the best for treatment. I needed to get a firm understanding of what I was dealing with. I needed clarity. I solved problems all the time in business and for my clients, so I did what I knew to do. I approached this health situation as a problem that needed a solution. Sitting around and feeling helpless wasn't an option. Fortunately, my finances at the time were such that I wasn't concerned about the money. I was willing to fly wherever I needed and do whatever was needed to get the best doctors involved.

In my spiritual life, a cancer diagnosis was another ton of bricks coming down on me. A ton of bricks that hit hard and raised questions about my faith, my trust. I called out to God for wisdom, help, and healing. I shed many tears and spent many days and nights alone, just me and God, locked in my room with my Bible. I said to Him, *"Okay, this is real. I need you to come through for me. I've been in church all my life, and I've heard many stories about other people being healed. But I've never faced anything like this before. And honestly, I don't understand what's happening to me. But, I'm not asking why because I know we live in a fallen world where s**t happens (pardon my language, but that's what I said. I wasn't in a mood to be fake or phony, I was totally transparent with Him), and this is the world we live in, so why not me? But I need to know if you are who I've* *been told you are. I need to know what your Word says about healing, and I need to really know it and understand it. I need you to reveal yourself to me in the area of healing."* With tears and a deep sense of sincerity and desperation, I picked up my Bible, and, starting with the book of Matthew, I reread the entire New Testament word for word. I was hungry to know, without a doubt, everything with respect to people who were sick and how Jesus handled it.

I told myself I was going to learn the "truth" about healing for real, and I would believe whatever the Bible said. I had already been a student and sponge concerning knowledge about health, nutrition, and natural remedies, and healing, and was applying a lot of what I'd learned. But here I was, looking and feeling more fit than ever, and hit with a cancer diagnosis. So I knew this was a situation requiring spiritual intervention for sure! I decided that, however, Jesus responded to sickness, disease, and healing, that's what I would adopt as *truth*. I would forget everything I had been taught or everything I'd heard others say up to that point. I was ready for a personal revelation, a personal understanding, a spiritual transformation based on my own revelation from God on this topic. And whatever it was, that would become my new mindset on healing. I was serious about this. I was so serious that I told God, "This is a make or break moment for me. I need to hear directly from you. And if you have nothing to say to me on the topic of this cancer diagnosis and my healing, if there's no revelation you choose to give me, I'll accept that as a signal to erase everything I thought I knew about the Bible, Christianity, and healing and move on to something else." I'm not recommending that you talk to God like that. I'm simply being totally transparent with you right now, as I was being totally transparent with Him at that moment because I felt with all of my being that I was *done* living by what other people said. I needed God to speak to me! I needed to know that He is real and that He heals! And if none of that was true, I need to know that!

This was no time for listening to other people tell me their opinions or what they had read or what they had heard about other people's experiences. I needed to know for myself. I was willing to throw out all preconceived notions and everything I had been told about healing up to that point and embrace *only* what was in the Scriptures that I had read for myself and whatever revelations and downloads the Holy Spirit was giving me during that time.

And here's what I found. I didn't see a *single* instance where Jesus failed to heal those who came to Him and asked for healing. Not *once* did He tell people, "You're not holy enough" or "You're not good enough" to be healed. The only scenario where He "couldn't do miracles" was when He was in a town where people doubted

and had no faith; and then He said He could do no miracles there, not because He didn't want to (*He did want
to!*), but because of their unbelief. Well, I did believe, so
that didn't apply to me.

For months, I prayed and believed for healing. I went
to my pastor and his wife, who was also one of my closest friends, and told them both what I was dealing with;
they prayed with me and laid hands on me, and anoint-
ed me with oil. I had faith! I went back for a second
round of tests, and the results showed that the cancer
was still there. I asked them to double-check because
I really expected them to say, "We don't understand it,
but the tumor is gone!" But that's not what they said.
Once again, I left the doctor's office in shock, not sure
how to feel or what to say.

The cancer was still there, and none of the non-inva-
sive laser surgeries I researched were applicable to my
case. Those treatments could only be done for noncan-
cerous tumors. So, as I sat in my room talking to God
and crying out for understanding, I believe He spoke
to me. And this is what I heard Him say, "*Joi, don't put
me in a box. Every good thing and every perfect thing comes
from me. Healing is good, in whatever form it comes, and healing is from me. So just believe. You're not in a position to tell
me how to heal you. Just accept the healing however I send
it.*" It was a calm yet deep and multi-dimensional voice
coming from a source with no boundaries, like a vast

ocean would sound if water could speak. That may seem weird, but that's what it sounded like. It brought tears to my eyes, and I felt so small in the presence of such a huge spiritual force. It was beautiful, and I remember thinking, *Wow, I wish every person who says there is no God could experience this.* There's no way they'd think He didn't exist if they felt and heard His presence the way that I did at that moment.

Feeling humbled and seeing at that moment how any other perspective was absolutely prideful and frankly ridiculous, I said, *"Okay, Lord. Yes, you're right. Everything that's good comes from you. And healing is certainly good. Thank you for opening my eyes to see you in a broader way and not limit you to my small way of thinking."* I felt a huge sense of relief that day. Up to that point, deep within, I was hoping to be one of those people who'd be able to stand up before my church congregation and say, "Look! God performed a miracle! I was diagnosed with cancer, but I prayed and went back to the doctor, and he said the tumor was miraculously gone! The cancer was gone! Praise God!" But when God told me not to put Him in a box and not to tell Him *how* to heal me, all I could do was bow and say, "Yes, Lord. Okay."

And I then proceeded to call my parents and siblings, had them all meet me at my parent's house at the same time, and I shared the news calmly and matter-of-factly with all of them. I told them what I had been diagnosed with, what I had found in my research in terms of survival rates and treatment options, my conversation with and revelation from the Lord, what my next steps would be, and how the surgery would be performed. (*By the way, one of the best doctors for performing thyroid removal surgery at the time happened to be in Chicago, thirty minutes from my house...what a Godsend! I had talked to surgeons at some of the best hospitals and cancer treatment centers across the U.S., and they unanimously agreed that the head of otolaryngology surgery at Northwestern Memorial was my best option. Note: otolaryngology is the oldest medical specialty in the U.S., dealing with disease and treatment of ear, nose, and throat issues. I had no idea what it was until my diagnosis.*) I calmly told my family, while looking around the table and seeing my sister's eyes get watery and my brother looking with this stunned look on his face, that I didn't want anyone crying or feeling sad for me. I was going to go through this, and I would come out fine on the other side. This was no time for tears. No time for fear. And no time for doubt. I explained to all of my family that this would be my last time talking about my health situation in detail because I didn't want to keep rehashing the facts or opening up a window for emotions to take over. I just wanted to fix my mind on the truth of God's Word and His promise to heal me. So I sat there and told them to ask all their questions so we could discuss, and after that, I was moving on and didn't want to talk about it again in detail. Honestly, I don't know how I was able to get through that conversation with all my family sitting around the table. It was as if a power not my own took over and was speaking through me, and that same power took control of my emotions and gave me such a peace that there was no room for sadness or fear. I know that it had to be God because I wouldn't have had that kind of strength or resolve on my own.

I admittedly had my moments of breaking down emotionally after that, as any normal human being would. Nobody likes the idea of having surgery, and especially when you've also been diagnosed with cancer. It's a lot to deal with. And the thought of having to take off work and not knowing what the recovery process would be like or what I would say to my clients and staff was very upsetting—especially considering that all of this was happening at a time when my business was in a growth spurt and needed my attention. But I knew I was doing the right thing to have the surgery and put this behind me. I had surgery. The tumor was removed; post-surgery the hospital staff told me that my case was the best possible scenario in terms of how the surgery went, which was smoothly and without a hitch. My recovery period and post-surgery results showed that all of the cancerous tissue was successfully removed. Because the thyroid is connected to the vocal cords, I had to undergo some vocal therapy to get my voice back. But that went well too.

To this day, I remain cancer-free! After going through that experience, there's nothing that anyone can ever tell me to persuade me that God doesn't heal or that He heals in just one specific way. I learned an important lesson through my cancer experience, as awful as it was to go through it. And that is that God is God, and we aren't Him! And He always fulfills His promises. We can trust Him!

His thoughts truly are higher than ours, and His ways truly are past our ability to understand with our human brains. But He definitely will talk to us if we come to Him with an open, believing heart. He'll reveal things to us about Himself. He showed me that what I had heard from many "Christians" who always said things like, "If you have faith, we can pray, and God will heal miraculously without the need for medication or surgery," was a limited perspective. And, perhaps more importantly, focusing solely on "the miraculous healing power of God" when a person is dealing with a health crisis often leaves the person feeling bad or like there's something wrong with him/her if they *do* need medication or surgery. While it is true, if we ask anything, believing, we can have what we ask (that's Scripture), I don't believe we can tell God *how* to answer our prayers. He always answers, but sometimes in ways that we don't necessarily understand or in ways that we wouldn't have considered. But when it comes to healing, people often put *their* perspectives into the mix and focus on how *they* want to see things work out. Not just from an outcome perspective, but in terms of what the whole process should look like. But who are we to tell God how to heal and expect Him to do it our way, exactly according to *our* view of what the process should look like?

I mean, after all, He sees the beginning and the end. He sees the whole picture of our lives and all the details from birth until death and beyond. And we only see the past and the present (that is, the part we're living in right now). Who knows better, Him or us? Hmmm. The truth is, every doctor, every person who invented a "cure" for something, all-natural remedies found in the earth, and yes, what we would consider today to be "miracle" healings, *all* come from God. There is no form of healing that doesn't come from Him. And *no* one method is "better" or "worse," nor is it a sign of how much or how little faith a person has.

Perhaps the most important thing I learned through this was what it looks like to truly trust God. How to walk through a dark valley in life when literally no other human can save you or protect you and, at that moment, to experience a peace like you've never known, and receive clarity and wisdom and guidance on the steps you need to take. All of that came solely from putting 100 percent of my trust in God. I'm so grateful that my eyes have been opened and my perspective expanded through this personal, deep experience with the Lord. I now know Him in a way that I probably never would have had I not gone through this experience and been diagnosed with cancer. But I stand on the other side of this, as well as a financial crisis, better equipped now than ever to help other people walk through similar situations. I'm able to tell them not what I've heard or observed in others but what I *know* to be true about God as provider and God as healer.

And here, on the other side of both of those situations, I have a deeper understanding of what it truly means to trust God. When your world comes crashing down, trust God. When you're facing powerful obstacles and villains that have come to destroy you, trust God. When nothing seems to make sense, trust God. When you don't know what to do, turn to God, seek His face, and immerse yourself deeply in His Word. Shut out *all* other voices but His. And I promise you, He will absolutely lead you and rescue you. Every time! He is, truly, the superhero above all others. And He's put super power inside of us to help us get through even the most difficult times.

I am still a work in progress. I don't profess, by any means, to say I fully know how trust works between humans and God, but I certainly do know it is an exchange.

Our trust in Him is an important "input" that results in Him pouring things into our lives so He can not only bless us, but so that He can bless others through us. Simply put, it's this formula for success:

Our trust in Him + His response = Blessings and power beyond what we can imagine

While these personal experiences I've shared were horrible in the moment, in terms of the struggle emotionally, financially, and health-wise (and in some cases relationship-wise), they were among the most pivotal moments in my life in terms of spiritual growth and my relationship with the Lord. I am grateful for what came out of those experiences. I urge anyone who is reading this to please think about, pray, and ask God to open your eyes to the reality of what you are putting your trust in. Ask Him to help you discern "real" from "fake" and to pull you out of the "matrix."

Ask yourself whether you, too, have fallen into a trap and bought into society's lie (or even "religious" lies) of what success is and how to achieve it. Are you putting your trust in this world's system? Even if you feel life is comfortable, from the world's standards, or that you're "doing all the right things" from a health or "religious" perspective, I challenge you to open up your mind to the possibility that, just maybe, the world's definition of success might be a lie. Even if you're a "believer" or Christian, there may be some false views you've acquired about being "immune" to certain things simply because you believe in God, attend church, tithe, or serve at church. Societal and "religious" perspectives and definitions of success might just be a hindrance to you reaching your full God-given potential and living your best life.

I believe that is *exactly* the case oftentimes. God has so much more for us, but we must be willing to open our minds and, many times, reject things we may have learned in the past from society (or even "religion"). Then, let Him reform, reshape, and renew our minds and how we think about Him, trust, other people, and things.

Ask yourself (and be honest): Have I put my trust in things? Have I put my trust in family or relationships with any other people (including my spouse, friends, or even spiritual leaders)? Have I been looking at my neighborhood or my bank account or my retirement accounts and feeling secure (or insecure) based on these things? Have I been relying on my knowledge of society's rules and dos and don'ts regarding how to be "healthy" to determine what I believe about healing and how I view my health? Because all these things can give us a false sense of security. There is no security outside of God. Zero. In Him is where our trust should be. He is not a person.

He will never fail us or go back on His promise. He is the only One who is capable of holding our trust. Now and in the future, He is faithful and trustworthy. He will never fail to show up and rescue you when you trust and believe in Him.

I have one practical action step for this chapter. It's simple yet powerful and transformative. If you answered yes to any of the questions in the previous paragraph, or if you know deep down on an intuitive level that you're playing small and not really trusting God completely, I invite you—right now—to do this one thing. Make a decision that, starting today, you'll embark on a personal journey to get to know God more deeply, more intimately. Because once you do, your automatic response to His awesomeness will be to love and trust Him more and more each day. And you'll discover that He is the ultimate "superhero" (and you have superhero power inside of you!)

CHAPTER 8

The Game Changer

I am the vine; you are the branches. If you remain in me and I in you, you will bear much fruit; apart from me you can do nothing.

John 15:5

I f you read nothing else but this chapter, know this—the following information can change your life *forever*, no matter what you're going through.

Life can be challenging and filled with difficult twists and turns to navigate. Life sometimes throws us curve balls and presents challenges that can shake us to the core. Sometimes we face situations that make us wonder, *How will I ever survive this?* Well, here's the truth of the matter, no matter what we face or how dark our paths can get at times, if we accept God's gift of salvation (by believing and confessing that Jesus died for our sins and God raised Him from the dead), we are guaranteed victory. That's right: guaranteed. We may not know all the twists and turns and challenges that are in our future, but we can know how the story ends. We are victorious! Just as Jesus was victorious in the end when He laid His life down on the cross and rose from the grave victorious, that same ending of "victory" is promised to us. And God never fails to deliver on His promise.

The only guaranteed path to true, sustained success in life is the one that God leads us down. According to the Bible, He leads us and guides us and, even in the lowest valleys or in times where we face our greatest enemies, He is always with us and provides for us (Psalm 23). He operates in the spirit realm, so we don't see Him with our physical eyes, but if we tune in and learn to tap into His Spirit within us, we can absolutely experience and feel Him.

According to Scripture, as Jesus is, so are we in this world. He was and is victorious, and so are we. We have great spiritual power inside of us. No matter what the circumstances in your relationships or life, in general, look like right now, it's not over. Put your faith in God and trust Him to lead you to victory. The story has been written, and we win! It's like in a movie when it looks like the bad guy is going to win, and then all of a sudden the plot changes, and the bad guy gets caught, and the good guy comes out on top at the end. Or a football game when the odds seemed stacked against a team, and there are minutes left in the last quarter, and somehow they pull it off and score a winning touch-down. That's how life sometimes is. It can seem as though we've lost and the game is ending, but God *always* comes through for His children and sees to it that we score and win the game in the end. How awesome is that? What's hard is not knowing *when* or *how* He's going to bring us the victory. But we can rest assured; there *is* a guaranteed victory once we put our faith and trust in Him.

The most important thing you can do is make a decision to accept the gift of salvation and be spiritually reborn into God's family. As a son or daughter of God, you will be assured victory in relationships, your health, your finances, and every area. This was a game-changer for me, and it can be for you too!

If you haven't made this decision but would like to, pray this simple prayer out loud:

"God, I believe that Jesus is your son, and you sent Him to earth to die for my sins. And I believe you raised Him from the dead so I could have victory in life. I accept your gift of salvation and ask Jesus to come into my heart as Lord and Savior. Thank you for saving me, for making me a new creature and putting your Spirit within me, and for making it possible for me to spend eternity with you in heaven. Take my life and use it for your purpose and to glorify you. In Jesus' name, I pray. Amen."

About the Author

—Joi M. Ross
Business Owner/Author/Communications
Consultant/Trainer

"She is committed to giving her time, talents, and resources to bring love and light to others."

Joi Ross is more than wit and humor. She is an author, trainer, coach, consultant, and CEO of Joi Ross Consulting. Her focus is helping others to identify and tap into their spiritual power, achieve abundance and freedom, and identify and remove limiting beliefs and mindsets that too often hold us back from fulfilling the dreams and visions we were created to achieve. Joi also founded and remains CEO of APEX Direct, a consulting firm focused on communications, training, and public education and outreach for government and private sector organizations.

Many years ago, after rejecting a life of "religious rules, dos, and don'ts," and going through a period of deep soul searching, Joi embraced a "non-religious" view of Christianity focused on a personal relationship with Jesus, God's grace, and love for mankind. It was during that time that she began giving counsel to people facing a variety of challenges, including financial difficulty, anxiety, fear, depression, and grief. She has actively volunteered and led various teams throughout her adult life, including serving on the Board of Directors for a women's shelter.

Joi holds a master's degree in public services management and a bachelor's degree in business with a minor in psychology. She's a lifelong learner and a lover of God and people. Those who know her well describe her as warm, kind, and down-to-earth. She is passionate about helping people on their journeys to grow spiritually, mentally, and emotionally, with a specific emphasis on mindset and transformational change from the inside out.

No matter which hat she's wearing or which way she chooses to serve, Joi Ross is a burning torch and a thought leader who effortlessly and resiliently *ignites the soul!*

https://JoiRoss.com
www.AlwaysPursuingExcellence.com
joi@joiross.com
Facebook: Joi Ross
   Joi Ross: www.facebook.com/joi.ross.77
   Joi Ross Consulting: www.facebook.com/
     JoiRossConsulting
Instagram: Joi Ross Consulting

Leave heartbreak behind, and thrive in any relationship! Start your journey today! Download my free guide, *Rethink Trust and Thrive*, at https://joiross.com/products.

CPSIA information can be obtained
at www.ICGtesting.com
Printed in the USA
BVHW040311210322
631575BV00004B/12